Cooking

'Round the Clock

RACHAEL RAY
30-MINUTE MEALS

by Rachael Ray

Lake Isle Press
New York

Published by:
Lake Isle Press, Inc.
16 West 32nd Street, Suite 10-B
New York, NY 10001
(212) 273-0796
E-mail: lakeisle@earthlink.net

Distributed to the trade by:
National Book Network (NBN), Inc.
4501 Forbes Boulevard, Suite 200
Lanham, MD 20706
1 (800) 462-6420
www.nbnbooks.com

Library of Congress Control Number: 2004113707

ISBN: 1-891105-16-7

Food photography: Courtesy of the Food Network

Book and cover design: Ellen Swandiak

This book is available at special sales discounts for bulk purchases as
premiums or special editions, including personalized covers. For more
information, contact the publisher at (212) 273-0796 or by e-mail,
lakeisle@earthlink.net

10 9

Special Thanks

Thank you, as always, to those who stand by me, around the clock: my family, friends, and co-workers and the wonderful, fun, and vocal fans of 30 Minute Meals!

~

Special thanks to the hardest-working woman in publishing, Hiroko Kiiffner, who works around the clock. You rock and I wouldn't change a page of our work together. (Well, just that one! Ha! Ha!)

~

Special thanks to Ellen for working around the clock on the design of this book and thanks to Pimpila for getting me through a hundred queries I didn't like answering.

~

Special thanks to my mom, Elsa, who continues to work around the clock with me and for me. I love eating with you (always too quickly) around the clock and around the world!

~

Special thanks to John for being such a good cook—for me! You make food fun, around the clock! Hoot-hoot! Ert! Ert!

I eat at all hours of the day and night.

I do everything around the clock, including work and play. Even as a baby, I would stay up all night. I didn't like milk or going to bed early. My grandpa Emmanuel would give me water and wine in my bottle. My cheeks would turn rosy and I would eventually go to sleep. Everyone in the family was tricked into thinking I was a good baby. My first word actually was "Vino!" I shouted it at the table as I raised my sippy cup. The jig was up.

As a toddler, and off the bottle, I was up again, all night. My dad took over the graveyard shift, watching cop shows with me. Mannix, Cannon, Ironside, McMillan and Wife, Columbo, and Banachek were all my good friends in prime time. By the time Charlie Chan and his sons appeared in the wee small hours, we'd be sharing leftovers and some cheese and olives.

Later, as a school kid, I was a real night crawler. I would get up and creep downstairs. I would make myself a snack (two or three courses) and settle in on the floor to draw pictures, read or write. I'd make posters, write stories and small books. I'd work three chapters ahead in schoolbooks. Sooner, but usually later, my mom would walk into the living room and see me there, sprawled out with my papers and pens and colors and dirty dishes. She'd put an end to my private party, forcing me to get at least a few winks in before school. Many nights I think she let me go on working for a few hours, because she knew that, at least in my own mind, I believed I was doing my best work.

Today, not much has changed. I do not have much time for cop shows anymore. But, I still stay up a good bit of the night. I often write between the hours of 10PM and dawn, with a panini or some killer salami scrambled eggs by my side. For me, even after a 10-hour day and another few hours in front of my computer, nothing satisfies me more than really good food, made with my own two hands.

From pizza to all-night diner eats, late-night romantic suppers to weekend brunches and fancy lunches, this collection of recipes is a real go-to resource to use at any hour of the day or night.

I try to organize my books in user-friendly ways. For example, chapters in my other books are designated as date meals, great eats for watching sports, and holiday dinners for 6 people or less. You don't have to search far for the perfect menu.

Knowing that hunger can strike almost anytime 24/7, I've organized this book by the hours of the day and night. In Rise & Shiners, you'll find energizing breakfasts, and in Late-Night Bites you'll find all-night diner foods to make right at home. Early-Bird Specials will make busy moms happy. And we've included recipe titles in the Table of Contents to help you scan chapter selections at a glance.

I can cook as fast as I can eat—and so can you! In fact, many of these recipes taste so good I am always caught between eating as fast as I can and trying to chew longer to make it last. (I know, pretty gross, but true.)

Bottom line: I may be sleep deprived, but these are the best 30-minutes-or-less meals for any hour of the day or night that you are going to find in one place! Stay up late, or get up early and get cooking! Are you hungry yet?

Rachael's Reminders

~ FIRST THINGS FIRST

Read each menu or recipe through before you begin. It's the best way to check out your ingredient list and familiarize yourself with the recipe steps, which are "layered" for convenience and time.

~ HOW TO MEASURE

As you may know, I am more relaxed about measurements than other cooks. Ingredients are called for in both measured and free-hand terms, e.g., 2 tablespoons extra-virgin olive oil or twice around the pan. Beginners need to measure, but eventually you will develop an eye and a feel for ingredients in quantity. You will discover that cooking is more art than science, and that you were born with the most important instruments of all, your hands and your palate. You will learn to trust them.

~ SHORTCUTS

There are times when store-bought items make sense. For example, I sometimes suggest pre-shredded cheeses and cut veggies as options. They spare the cook and offer convenience that's hard to beat.

~ SUBSTITUTIONS

About altered or reduced-fat products. Personally I rarely use them, but that's your decision entirely. Substitute freely, as you like or need to. If you prefer reduced-fat cheese and dairy products, the consistencies of dips, spreads or sauces may be slightly thinner. In any case, always season to taste.

~ YOU ARE NOT RACING THE CLOCK

You're taking only 30 minutes out of your day to prepare a welcoming meal for yourself and your family. More importantly, you are creating a chance to relax and spend time with people you love. What could be better than that!

Table of Contents

RISE
7 to 11
& SHINERS

SCRAMBLES

MENU A CHAMPAGNE TOAST

HASH IT OUT

DESSERT FOR BREAKFAST

A QUINTESSENTIAL CONTINENTAL

HEARTY OPENERS

LET'S DO 11 to 4 LUNCH

EARLY-BIRD 4 to 7 SPECIALS

SIT-DOWN 7 to 9 SUPPERS

TV DINNERS & SNACKS

7 to 12

BISTRO
9 to 12
MEALS

I love breakfasts. Start the day with any of these fabulous scrambles, a fancy Vanilla-Almond French Toast, Cowboy Hash, scones and more. Yum!

COOKING 'ROUND THE CLOCK

RISE & SHINERS

7 to 11

RACHAEL RAY 30-MINUTE MEALS

Even simpler than making omelets or frittatas, I make scrambles: jumbles of different vegetables and meats mixed into scrambled eggs. I have also included a selection of scrambles in the Late Night section of this book made from ingredients many of us keep on hand.

SCRAMBLES

~ GREEN EGGS AND HAM WITH ITAL-TOTS AND GARLIC-CHEESY TOAST

~ SCRAMBLES WITH SALMON AND PEAS

~ SARDOU SCRAMBLE

~ SAUSAGE SCRAMBLES AND CHEESE

~ TURKEY PASTRAMI SCRAMBLES ON RYE

~ BACON SCRAMBLES, SPINACH, AND TOMATO ON TOAST

~ JOHN'S GOURMET SCRAMBLES FOR RACHAEL

Green Eggs and Ham with Ital-Tots and Garlic-Cheesy Toast

My friend Wade gave me a copy of Dr. Seuss's "Green Eggs and Ham" in Italian: "Uova Verde con Prosciutto." I absolutely treasure it! Another friend, Jon Young, a chef in Chicago, made me a fabulous breakfast of his green eggs and ham once, and I have seen them on a few other menus since. This is my home version of Jon's eggs, done Italian style, in tribute to Wade. (I think both would approve!)

ITAL-TOTS

1 sack frozen **tater tots,** any brand

1 teaspoon **salt**

1 teaspoon dried **thyme**

1 teaspoon dried **oregano**

1 teaspoon dried **rosemary**

1 teaspoon crushed hot **red pepper flakes**

GREEN SAUCE

1/2 cup baby **spinach** or arugula leaves (2 handfuls)

10-12 fresh **basil** leaves (about 1/2 cup)

2 tablespoons **pine nuts** (pignoli) (a palmful)

1 small clove **garlic,** cracked from skin

Salt and freshly ground black **pepper,** to taste

2 rounded spoonfuls grated **Parmigiano** Reggiano or Romano cheese

1/4 cup **extra-virgin olive oil** (evoo) (eyeball it)

EGGS AND HAM

1 tablespoon **extra-virgin olive oil** (evoo) (once around the pan)

1 tablespoon **butter**

1/2 pound breakfast **ham**, chopped

8 large **eggs**

A splash of **half-and-half** or milk

Salt and freshly ground black **pepper**

TOAST

4 thick slices crusty Italian **bread**

1 clove **garlic**, cracked from skin

Butter, for bread

Grated **Parmigiano** Reggiano or Romano cheese, for sprinkling

Make the Ital-tots: Preheat oven to 425°F. Open tots bag and pour four portions onto a nonstick cookie sheet. Sprinkle the tots with salt and dried seasonings and toss them around a bit to get the herbs to stick to the tots. Bake the tots until crisp, about 12 minutes. Remove from oven and switch the broiler on.

Make the green sauce: Combine ingredients in a food processor and process until sauce forms. Set sauce aside and reserve.

Prepare the eggs and ham: Heat a medium nonstick skillet over medium-high heat. Add evoo and butter to pan, then add the chopped ham and cook to lightly brown at edges, 3 minutes or so.

Beat eggs and half-and-half or milk with salt and pepper. Add eggs to ham in the skillet and scramble them up with the ham to desired doneness and remove from heat.

Make the toast: Toast bread under hot broiler, 30 seconds on each side. Rub with cracked garlic then spread with butter and top with a sprinkle of cheese.

Stir the green sauce into the ham and eggs, and serve with Ital-tots and Garlic-Cheesy Toast on the side.

YIELD: 4 SERVINGS

Scrambles with Salmon and Peas

8 large **eggs**
3 tablespoons **herb cheese**, Boursin or Alouette, cut into bits
2 tablespoons chopped fresh **chives**
2 tablespoons chopped fresh **dill**
Salt and freshly ground black **pepper**
2 tablespoons **butter**
1/2 cup frozen green **peas** (a couple of handfuls)
1/4 pound **smoked salmon**, cut into small pieces or strips
Buttered toasted **pumpernickel** bread, to pass at table

Heat a medium nonstick skillet over medium heat. Whisk together eggs, cheese, chives, dill, salt, and pepper. Melt butter in the skillet and add egg mixture. Scramble until eggs are still soft but taking shape. Add peas and salmon and finish cooking, about 1 minute longer. Serve with toasted pumpernickel bread.

YIELD: 4 SERVINGS

Sardou Scramble

1 box (10 ounces) frozen chopped **spinach**
1 can (15 ounces) **artichoke hearts** in water, drained
2 tablespoons **extra-virgin olive oil** (evoo) (twice around the pan)
1/4 small **onion**, finely chopped (about 3 tablespoons)
8 large **eggs**
3 tablespoons **herb cheese**, Boursin or Alouette, cut into bits
Salt and freshly ground black **pepper**
Buttered toasted **wheat bread,** to pass at table

Defrost spinach in the microwave. Drain off liquid. Place spinach in a clean kitchen towel and wring out the spinach until it is dry. Loosen the spinach with your fingertips on a cutting board or in a small bowl. Chop the artichoke hearts into small pieces.

Heat a medium nonstick skillet over medium heat. Add evoo, then add onions. One minute later, stir in the spinach and artichokes.

Beat eggs with cheese, salt, and pepper. Add eggs to spinach and artichokes. Scramble to the desired doneness and serve with buttered wheat toast.

YIELD: 4 SERVINGS

Sausage Scrambles and Cheese

1 tablespoon **extra-virgin olive oil** (evoo) or vegetable oil (once around the pan)

1 pound bulk **breakfast sausage,** such as maple sausage

8 large **eggs**

A splash of **half–and-half** or whole milk

A few drops **hot sauce,** such as Tabasco

Salt and freshly ground black **pepper**

1/3 pound **cheddar** cheese, diced

1 plum **tomato,** seeded and diced

Buttered toasted **whole-grain bread** with honey, to pass at table

Heat a medium nonstick skillet over medium-high heat. Add evoo or vegetable oil; add sausage and cook, crumbling the meat, until brown, 5 or 6 minutes. Remove sausage from the pan and drain off some of the fat. Return pan to heat and reduce the temperature to medium-low.

Whisk together eggs, half-and-half or milk, hot sauce, salt, and pepper. Scramble eggs until just soft, then add cheese and continue to scramble another minute or so to finish cooking eggs and to begin to melt the cheese bits. Remove pan from heat and combine sausage and eggs. Serve plates of sausage scrambles garnished with a few pieces of diced fresh tomato and with toast with honey on the side.

YIELD: 4 SERVINGS

Turkey Pastrami Scrambles on Rye

2 tablespoons **butter** or extra-virgin olive oil (evoo)

1/2 pound deli-sliced **turkey pastrami**, chopped

8 large **eggs**, beaten

Salt and freshly ground black **pepper**

1 teaspoon **paprika**

1 teaspoon **hot sauce**, such as Tabasco

2 tablespoons chopped or snipped **chives**

Brown, spicy **mustard** (optional)

4 slices **rye bread**, toasted

Heat a medium nonstick skillet over medium heat. Add butter and let it melt. Add pastrami and cook 2 or 3 minutes.

Beat eggs together with salt, pepper, paprika, hot sauce, and chives. Add to pastrami and scramble eggs and meat together.

To serve, spread mustard, if desired, on the rye toast. Place a slice of toast on each plate and top with pastrami scrambles, making open-faced sandwiches.

YIELD: 4 SERVINGS

Bacon Scrambles, Spinach, and Tomato on Toast

1 tablespoon **extra-virgin olive oil** (evoo) (once around the pan)

4 slices applewood-smoked **bacon**, chopped

8 large **eggs**, beaten

1 teaspoon **hot sauce**, such as Tabasco

Salt and freshly ground black **pepper**

1/4 pound fresh baby **spinach** leaves (a couple of handfuls), chopped

2 tablespoons **butter**, softened

1 teaspoon spicy **mustard**

4 slices white or wheat **bread**, toasted

1 vine-ripened **tomato**, thinly sliced

Heat a medium nonstick skillet over medium-high heat. Add evoo and the chopped bacon. Brown bacon pieces for 3 or 4 minutes. Drain off a little of the fat. Season beaten eggs with hot sauce, salt, and pepper. Scramble eggs with bacon in the pan. When eggs are almost to the consistency that you like, add the chopped spinach and wilt the leaves into eggs.

Combine butter and mustard. Spread the mixture on warm toast. Place a piece of mustard-buttered toast on each plate and top with mounds of bacon and spinach egg scrambles. Top the open-faced sandwiches with thin slices of tomato and serve.

YIELD: 4 SERVINGS

John's Gourmet Scrambles for Rachael

This is my favorite scrambles recipe because John, my true love, made it up just for me. (He is as tasty as these eggs!) Truffle oil, John's not-so-secret ingredient, is widely available in many larger markets with gourmet aisles or sections. Try drizzling it on pasta, vegetables, rice, or risotto—even on hot, crusty bread. You'll be amazed at how easily this added layer of wild mushroom flavor can turn everyday staples into gourmet morsels! Written for two, try this recipe as a breakfast-in-bed treat for your sweetie.

6 large **eggs**
Salt and freshly ground black **pepper**
1/2 teaspoon (a few dashes) **hot sauce**, such as Tabasco
1 teaspoon **truffle oil** or white truffle oil (eyeball it, a good drizzle)
2 tablespoons chopped or snipped **fresh** chives
3 tablespoons **herb cheese**, Boursin or Alouette, cut into bits
2 tablespoons **butter**
1 plum **tomato**, seeded and finely diced
2 slices **whole-grain bread**, toasted

Heat a medium nonstick pan over medium heat. Whisk eggs together with salt, pepper, hot sauce, truffle oil, chives, and herb cheese. Add butter to pan and let it melt. Add eggs and scramble to desired consistency. Serve eggs garnished with diced fresh tomato and a slice of whole-grain toast on the side.

YIELD: 2 SERVINGS

Next time a special occasion for a special someone comes up, cook this meal! It is perfect for wedding parties, anniversaries, birthdays, Mother's or Father's Day, or just to say "I love you" any day.

MENU A CHAMPAGNE TOAST

~ CRUNCHY VANILLA-ALMOND FRENCH TOAST WITH FANCY FRUIT TOPPING

~ SWEET 'N SMOKY BACON

~ GRAND MIMOSAS

Crunchy Vanilla-Almond French Toast with Fancy Fruit Topping and Sweet 'n Smoky Bacon

BACON

1 pound applewood-smoked **bacon**

1/2 cup firmly packed **dark-brown sugar**

TOAST

8 large **eggs**

1 cup **half-and-half**

2 teaspoons **vanilla extract**

2 pinches **salt**

1/2 teaspoon ground or freshly grated **nutmeg**

2 teaspoons ground **cinnamon**

3 cups **corn flakes**, lightly crushed

1/2 cup sliced **almonds**, lightly crushed

1/4 cup (1/2 stick) **butter**

12 (1 & 1/2-inch-thick) slices **challah** bread or soft Italian-style bread

Medium or dark amber **maple syrup**, to pass at table

Fresh **mint** sprigs, for garnish (optional)

Fresh **edible flowers**, for garnish (optional)

FRUIT TOPPING

1 large navel **orange**, peeled and chopped

12 large **strawberries**, hulled and sliced

1/2 pint **blueberries**

1/2 pint **raspberries**

1/2 pint **blackberries**

2 tablespoons **sugar**

1/4 cup **Grand Marnier** or other orange liqueur

Preheat oven to 350°F.

Prepare the bacon: Arrange bacon on a slotted broiler pan. Sprinkle with

brown sugar and place in oven to bake until crisp, 20 to 22 minutes.

Make the French toast: Heat a large nonstick skillet over medium heat. In a shallow dish, use a wire whisk to beat together eggs, half-and-half, vanilla, salt, nutmeg, and cinnamon. In a second shallow dish combine corn flakes and almonds. Add 2 tablespoons butter to warm skillet. Line a cookie sheet with aluminum foil and place near the stove. Coat 4 to 6 slices (depending on the size of your skillet) of bread in egg, then coat bread in corn flakes and nuts. Cook slices 2 minutes on each side and transfer toast to cookie sheet. Repeat with remaining slices. Place toast in oven while bacon is still cooking and bake 10 minutes.

Meanwhile, make the topping: Combine fruit, sugar, and liqueur in a serving bowl and reserve.

Remove toast and bacon from oven. Warm maple syrup in a small pitcher in the microwave, 15 seconds on high. Serve toast and bacon on plates garnished with mint and edible flowers, if desired. Pass syrup and fruit topping on the side.

YIELD: 6 SERVINGS

Grand Mimosas

6 tablespoons Grand Marnier or other orange liqueur
1 bottle brut champagne or sparkling wine, chilled
1/2 quart orange juice

To each champagne flute, add 1 tablespoon Grand Marnier. Add champagne to fill 2/3 of each flute. Top glasses off with orange juice. Serve.

YIELD: 6 SERVINGS

Similar to scrambles, my hashes are easy-to-make jumbles of meats and vegetables combined with eggs. What's the difference? The hashes are heavy on the jumbled ingredients and easy on the eggs; 1 large egg per serving.

HASH IT OUT

~ COWBOY HASH AND EGGS, TEXAS TOAST AND SALSA

~ BREAKFAST POLENTA AND ITALIAN HASH

~ GREEK HASH

Cowboy Hash and Eggs, Texas Toast and Salsa

HASH, EGGS, AND TEXAS TOAST

12 medium **mushrooms**, quartered

1 **green bell pepper**, seeded and diced

1/2 medium **red onion**, chopped

8 small red **potatoes**

3 slices applewood- or hickory-smoked **bacon**, chopped

2 tablespoons **extra-virgin olive oil** (evoo) (twice around the pan)

2 teaspoons **grill seasoning**, such as Montreal Steak Seasoning, or salt and freshly ground black pepper

Hot sauce, such as Tabasco, to taste

2 cups (8 ounces) shredded sharp **cheddar**, pepper-Jack, or smoked cheddar cheese

3 tablespoons **butter**

4 extra-large **eggs**

4 thick-cut slices white, whole wheat, or crusty farmhouse **bread**, 1 to 1 & 1/2 inches thick

1 clove **garlic**, cracked from skin

1/2 teaspoon **cayenne pepper** or several drops Tabasco

Chopped fresh flat-leaf **parsley**, for garnish

YELLOW TOMATO SALSA

Any flavor or variety of store-bought salsa is a fine substitute here.

3 medium or 2 large **yellow tomatoes**, seeded and chopped

1/2 medium **red onion**, finely chopped

1 serrano or **jalapeño** pepper, seeded and finely chopped

2 tablespoons chopped fresh **cilantro** or parsley

Salt, to taste

Make the hash: Chop all veggies. Pierce potatoes with a fork and microwave on high for 5 minutes. Remove potatoes from microwave and cool 5 minutes to handle.

While potatoes are working, add chopped bacon to a large skillet over medium-high heat and brown until crisp. Remove to paper towels to drain; wipe pan and return to heat.

Preheat the broiler to high.

Chop or wedge potatoes. Add evoo to the skillet you cooked the bacon in, then add potatoes. Cook potatoes until brown and crisp, 2 minutes on each side.

Make the salsa: Combine ingredients in a small bowl.

Back to the hash: Add mushrooms to potatoes. Brown mushrooms 1 or 2 minutes, then add peppers and onions and season mixture with grill seasoning blend or salt and pepper, then hot sauce. Cook until veggies are just tender and potatoes are cooked through, 3 to 5 minutes longer. Turn off heat and add bacon back to the pan. Combine bacon with the veggies then add cheese to the pan to evenly cover the mixture. Tent the skillet with aluminum foil to gently melt cheese over vegetables and potatoes and to retain heat.

Fry the eggs: Heat a nonstick griddle pan over medium heat. Add about 1 tablespoon butter to warm pan and let it melt. Crack eggs onto griddle and fry to desired doneness. Eggs may, of course, be cooked over easy or scrambled as well—as you like.

Make the toast: Place bread slices under broiler and toast 6 inches from heat on both sides. Place 2 tablespoons butter in a small cup with a clove of garlic and the cayenne pepper or a few drops of hot sauce. Melt in microwave 30 seconds. Brush toast with garlic cayenne butter and sprinkle with parsley.

Transfer vegetable and bacon hash to plates. Top each portion with a single fried egg or arrange the eggs evenly over the platter. Serve with Texas garlic toast and serve the salsa on the side.

YIELD: 4 SERVINGS

INSIDE SCOOP

One of my favorite restaurant breakfast meals is a "Morning Ray" at a restaurant of the same name in Park City, Utah. This is my at-home version—I should call it the "Morning Rachael Ray!" When in Park City, eat at Morning Ray. When you are at home, make this instead. For a vegetarian version, omit the bacon and substitute pan-fried tofu for eggs.

Breakfast Polenta and Italian Hash

4 tablespoons **extra-virgin olive oil** (evoo)

1 medium **onion**, chopped

1 **red bell pepper**, seeded and chopped

1/2 pound crimini **mushrooms**

Salt and freshly ground black **pepper**, to taste

3 cups **chicken broth**

1/2 pound deli-sliced **capicolla** (hot Italian ham), chopped

1 cup **cornmeal** or instant polenta

2 tablespoons **butter**, cut into small pieces

1/3 cup **Parmigiano** Reggiano or Romano cheese (a couple of handfuls)

4 large to extra-large **eggs**

A splash of **milk** or cream

1 tablespoon chopped fresh flat-leaf **parsley**

Heat a medium skillet over medium-high heat. Add 2 tablespoons evoo (twice around the pan). Add onions, peppers, and mushrooms and season with salt and pepper.

In a medium saucepan bring chicken broth to a boil. When broth boils, add ham to the vegetables, then add cornmeal or polenta to the broth, stirring, in a slow, even stream. Stir polenta while it thickens, 2 minutes. Remove from heat and stir in butter and cheese and season with salt and pepper.

Drop big spoonfuls of polenta onto individual plates or a platter. Top with ham and vegetables. Place loose aluminum foil over the top to keep veggies and polenta hot. Return veggie pan to the heat and add remaining evoo. In a bowl, beat eggs with milk or cream and salt, pepper, and parsley. Add eggs to pan and scramble to desired doneness, 1 to 3 minutes. Top hash with eggs and serve.

YIELD: 4 SERVINGS

Greek Hash

2 medium red **potatoes** or small white potatoes

2 tablespoons **extra-virgin olive oil** (evoo) (twice around the pan)

1 medium **onion,** chopped

1 **red bell pepper,** seeded and chopped

10 **sun-dried tomatoes** in olive oil, drained and chopped

1/4 cup pitted Kalamata **olives** (a handful), chopped

Salt and freshly ground black **pepper,** to taste

1 teaspoon dried **oregano** or 1 tablespoon chopped fresh oregano

A handful of fresh flat-leaf **parsley** leaves, chopped

1 package (1 pound) triple-washed **spinach** leaves, coarsely chopped

3/4 pound **feta** cheese, crumbled

2 tablespoons **butter**

4 large or extra-large **eggs,** beaten

Poke several holes in the potatoes with a fork. Microwave them on high for 5 minutes. Remove from microwave and cool, then dice.

Heat a large nonstick skillet over medium-high heat. Add evoo, diced potatoes, onions, bell peppers, sun-dried tomatoes, and olives. Season with salt and pepper and oregano and cook 10 minutes, turning hash occasionally. Add parsley and spinach to hash and fold in until spinach leaves wilt. Adjust seasonings. Turn off stove and leave hash in pan. Add crumbled feta to hash and let it sit so it begins to melt.

Heat a second medium skillet over medium heat. Add butter and let it melt. Add eggs and scramble to desired doneness. To serve, pile hash on plates and top with a heaping spoonful of scrambled eggs.

YIELD: 4 SERVINGS

I hate to measure, so I don't bake or make pancakes or waffles much. Still, there are a few recipes that I've learned from my mom and sister that are so amazing that I force myself to take the time to suffer through the measuring part. The next two recipes are among them.

DESSERT FOR BREAKFAST

~ GINGERBREAD WAFFLES

~ OATMEAL COOKIE PANCAKES

~ TOFFEE HOT CHOCOLATE

Gingerbread Waffles

I love warm gingerbread! With these waffles, I can have dessert for breakfast. This recipe makes four 4-section waffles. In my family everyone wants a whole four-section waffle to themselves, but our eyes are usually bigger than our stomachs.

3 cups all-purpose **flour**

4 teaspoons **baking powder**

2 teaspoons **cinnamon**

2 teaspoons ground **ginger**

1/2 teaspoon ground **nutmeg**

1/2 teaspoon **salt**

4 large **eggs**

2/3 cup firmly packed **brown sugar**

1 cup canned **pumpkin purée**

1 & 1/4 cups whole **milk**

1/2 cup **molasses**

1/2 cup (1 stick) **butter**, melted, plus additional tablespoon for the waffle iron

Warm **maple syrup**, to pass at table

Preheat waffle iron.

In a large bowl, combine flour, baking powder, cinnamon, ginger, nutmeg, and salt. In a medium bowl, beat eggs and brown sugar until fluffy, then beat in pumpkin, milk, molasses, and 1/2 cup melted butter. Stir the wet ingredients into the dry until just moist. Do not overstir the waffle batter. Brush the waffle iron with the remaining tablespoon melted butter to coat. Pour batter onto hot waffle iron and bake until golden brown. Repeat with remaining batter. Serve waffles with warm syrup.

YIELD: 4 TO 8 SERVINGS (FOUR 4-SECTION WAFFLES)

Oatmeal Cookie Pancakes

More dessert for breakfast: These pancakes taste just like giant oatmeal cookies. I recommend serving them with big glasses of ice-cold milk.

1 cup old-fashioned **oats**

1 cup all-purpose **flour**

1/2 cup firmly packed **brown sugar**

2 teaspoons **baking powder**

1/2 teaspoon **baking soda**

1 teaspoon **cinnamon**

2 ounces (1/4 cup) chopped **walnuts**

3/4 cup **sour cream**

3/4 cup whole **milk**

2 large **eggs**

1 teaspoon **vanilla** extract

2 really ripe **bananas**, mashed up

3/4 cup **raisins**

1/4 cup (1/2 stick) **butter**, melted, plus additional for skillet

Maple syrup or honey, for drizzling

Mix oats, flour, brown sugar, baking powder, baking soda, cinnamon, and walnuts in a medium bowl. In another large bowl, combine sour cream, milk, eggs, and vanilla. Whisk the dry ingredients into the wet until just combined, then fold in the mashed-up bananas and the raisins. Stir in the 1/4 cup melted butter.

Heat a griddle over medium heat and brush with additional melted butter. Pour about 1/3 cup batter for each pancake onto the griddle and cook until bubbles form on the top, about 2 minutes, then turn. Cook until golden brown on the other side, about 2 minutes.

YIELD: 4 SERVINGS; ABOUT TWELVE 5-INCH CAKES

Toffee Hot Chocolate

This is a rich morning drink, but it's equally perfect when you come in from sledding, skiing, or skating on cold winter days. As an afternoon treat, I would serve the drink with gingersnaps or molasses cookies for dunking.

4 cups whole **milk**
1/2 cup **water**
1/2 cup **sugar**
6 ounces bittersweet **chocolate**, chopped
2 ounces **butterscotch chips** (available on baking aisle)
1 canister **whipped cream** (available on dairy aisle)
1 **toffee bar**, such as Heath brand, crushed

Heat milk, water, and sugar to a boil, then remove from heat and stir in chocolate and butterscotch chips until they melt into the milk. Pour into small mugs or cups and top with whipped cream and crushed toffee pieces.

YIELD: 4 SERVINGS

A QUINTESSENTIAL CONTINENTAL

~ **ORANGE AND ALMOND SCONES**

~ **HAM AND CHEESE SCONES**

~ **JIMMY'S CORNBREAD MUFFINS FOR MORGAN**

Try any of these tasty breads-as-breakfast treats with juice and coffee or tea for a quintessential continental.

Orange and Almond Scones

1 box Jiffy brand **biscuit mix**

2 tablespoons **sugar**

1/2 cup **heavy cream**

Zest of 1 **orange**

1/4 cup sliced **almonds**, lightly crushed

1/4 teaspoon **almond extract** (a couple of drops)

Butter, to pass at table

Orange **marmalade**, to pass at table

Preheat oven to 375°F.

Mix together biscuit mix, sugar, cream, orange zest, almonds, and almond extract. Pile the mixture into 4 mounds for large scones or 8 for very small scones on a nonstick cookie sheet. Bake until light golden, 10 to 12 minutes for large scones, 7 to 8 minutes for small scones. Serve with butter and marmalade.

YIELD: 4 SERVINGS

Ham and Cheese Scones

1 box Jiffy brand **biscuit mix**

4 blades **chives**, chopped or snipped (2 tablespoons)

1/2 cup **heavy cream**

A couple pinches of **salt**

2 slices (1/8 pound) sliced baked or boiled **ham**, chopped

1/8 pound sharp **cheddar** cheese, diced into small pieces (1/4 cup)

Honey or honey mustard, to pass at table

Preheat oven to 375°F.

Mix together biscuit mix, chives, cream, salt, ham, and cheese. Pile mixture into 4 large mounds or 8 small mounds on a nonstick cookie sheet. Bake 10 to 12 minutes for large scones, 7 to 8 minutes for small scones. Serve with honey or honey mustard.

YIELD: 4 SERVINGS

Jimmy's Cornbread Muffins for Morgan

1 & 1/4 cups self-rising cornmeal (5 parts)

1/4 cup self-rising flour (1 part)

1/2 cup sugar (2 parts)

1 teaspoon salt

2 tablespoons freshly ground black pepper

1/2 cup (+ or -) buttermilk

Butter, to pass at table

Honey, to pass at table

Preheat the oven to 430°F with two 6-cup (or one 12-cup) medium muffin tins inside.

Combine cornmeal, flour, sugar, salt, and pepper. Stir in buttermilk until batter has consistency of thick cake batter.

Pour mixture into hot tins so cups are 3/4 full and bake 18 to 20 minutes. Switch oven to broil and broil on high until muffins reach desired brownness, 2 to 4 minutes.

YIELD: 12 MUFFINS

Recipe, courtesy of Jimmy Hays

So, in my work on Inside Dish—a fantastic show I am working on for the Food Network in which I eat and "dish" with famous actors and celebrities (I know: I am a lucky stinker!)—I met one of the most distinguished American stars, Morgan Freeman, a man of great character and class.

We taped the show at his blues club, Ground Zero—so named because it is located in Clarksdale, Mississippi, birthplace of the blues and where Mr. Robert Johnson is said to have sold his soul to the devil. There we were on this crowded floor dancing the hoochy-coo to Mustang Sally. Morgan's business partner Bill Luckett and his wife were there, too. Mrs. L. didn't seem to feel much like hoochy-cooing, so she stood off to the side of the dance floor looking lovely but a little lonely. Morgan walked away from all the cameras, up to this fine lady. He took her in his arms and danced a stardust waltz, nice and easy, to his own tempo. She glowed!

When we were done, a crowd of folks piled in, many of them Morgan's personal friends. One of them, Mr. Jimmy Hayes, revealed that he made cornbread for Morgan and his wife all the time. Non-baker that I am, I asked for the recipe.

Jimmy swore I wouldn't have to measure to make this recipe (my primary reason for avoiding baking altogether), and I didn't! I made them with lots of pepper, as instructed by Jimmy, and I ate the muffins with butter and honey—UNREAL!

If you're confident, you can eyeball rather than measure a lot of this recipe, too.

HEARTY OPENERS

~ COLD MORNING OATMEAL

~ HAM STEAKS WITH CURRIED FRUIT

~ CINNAMON-RAISIN TOAST STACKS WITH
EGGS AND BACON

Cold Morning Oatmeal

I live on a mountain in a very cold region of the Northeast. This breakfast is more than cozy and filling: On harsh winter mornings it becomes essential.

2 Macintosh **apples**

2 cups **apple cider**

2 cups **water**

2 pinches **salt**

1 teaspoon **cinnamon**

A handful of **golden raisins** or dried sweetened cranberries

2 cups instant **oats**

1/4 cup chopped **walnuts** or pecans

2 tablespoons **butter**

Pure **maple syrup,** for drizzling

Peel apples, cut them into quarters, and trim away seeds and core. Shred the apples with a grater into a medium saucepan. Add cider, water, salt, cinnamon, and raisins or cranberries. Bring the mixture to a boil and stir in instant oats. Remove the oatmeal from heat and continue to stir to thicken. Serve oatmeal in bowls and top with nuts, pats of butter, and a drizzle of maple syrup.

YIELD: 4 SERVINGS

Ham Steaks with Curried Fruit

This is a hearty and spicy breakfast. It's a recipe of my mama's.
(She's spicy, too.) I like it with hot chai (Indian tea with hot milk).

3 tablespoons **butter**

3/4 cup firmly packed **brown sugar**

1 tablespoon **curry powder**

1/2 fresh, cored **pineapple** (available in produce department),
   diced

2 **plums,** pitted and chopped

1 can (15 ounces) **apricots,** peaches, or pears in natural juice,
   drained and chopped

2 packages (1 pound each) **ham steak**

A drizzle of any light-colored **oil,** such as vegetable oil

Combine butter, sugar, and curry in a small pot over medium heat. Allow
sugar to bubble and melt into butter. Add fruit and cook 15 minutes,
stirring to coat fruit in sauce.

Remove ham steaks from package and pat dry. Heat a medium nonstick
skillet or griddle pan over medium-high heat. Drizzle pan with oil and fry
the ham steaks 5 minutes on each side. Serve ham topped with curried
fruit.

YIELD: 4 SERVINGS

Cinnamon-Raisin Toast Stacks with Eggs and Bacon

A Breakfast Club sandwich supreme.

6 slices applewood-smoked **bacon**
3 tablespoons **sugar**
1 teaspoon **cinnamon**
1/4 teaspoon ground **nutmeg**
6 slices **cinnamon-raisin swirl bread**, such as Sun-Maid brand
1/4 cup (1/2 stick) **butter**
8 large **eggs**
A splash of **milk** or cream
Salt and freshly ground black **pepper**
4 **bamboo skewers** (6 to 8 inches)

Preheat the broiler to high. Cut bacon slices in half and arrange the 12 pieces on a slotted broiler pan; cook 12 inches from broiler until crisp, 3 or 4 minutes on each side, then remove from oven. Leave the broiler on.

Mix sugar with cinnamon and nutmeg. Place bread on a baking sheet and put it in the oven, 12 inches from the broiler; toast until evenly golden on each side, about 2 minutes on the first side, 1 minute on the reverse. Butter each slice and sprinkle with cinnamon sugar.

Beat eggs with a splash of milk or cream, and salt and pepper. Heat a medium nonstick skillet over medium heat. Melt 2 tablespoons butter in the skillet and add the eggs. Cook eggs, scrambling, to desired doneness.

To assemble a Breakfast Club: Place a slice of cinnamon toast on a work surface, sugared side up. Top toast with a quarter of the scrambled eggs and 3 pieces of bacon, then another slice of toast, more eggs another 3 pieces bacon and another slice of cinnamon toast on top, sugared side down. Place 2 skewers in the bread to secure the club, and cut the sandwich in half, corner to corner. Each half sandwich is a full portion. Place the Breakfast Clubs on individual plates and serve.

YIELD: 4 SERVINGS

Lunch favorites with a twist. Try these super sammies, salads, and healthy veggie combos. You'll never go back to PB & J sandwiches!

COOKING 'ROUND THE CLOCK

LET'S DO **11 to 4** LUNCH

RACHAEL RAY 30-MINUTE MEALS

MENU BIG FLAVOR BRUNCH

~ PASTA SALAD WITH LEMON-PESTO DRESSING

~ SWEET ITALIAN CHICKEN-SAUSAGE PATTIES ·

~ BIRDS IN A NEST

Pasta Salad with Lemon-Pesto Dressing

Salt and freshly ground black **pepper,** to taste

1 cup store-bought **pesto sauce** (available in refrigerated section)

Grated zest and juice of 1 **lemon**

1/4 cup chopped fresh flat-leaf **parsley**

1 cup grape **tomatoes,** halved

4 **scallions,** chopped

20 fresh **basil** leaves, torn or cut into thin strips

3/4 pound **ricotta salata,** chopped and crumbled (available in specialty cheese case) or 1 (1-pound) tub bocconcini (mini balls of mozzarella), drained and halved

1 pound **cavatappi** or other corkscrew pasta or medium shells

Bring a large pot of water to a boil and salt it.

Make the dressing: Place pesto, lemon zest, lemon juice, parsley, tomatoes, scallions, basil, and cheese in a large bowl.

Cook pasta to al dente, then drain and chill it down under cold running water. Drain well. Add to bowl with dressing. Combine and season with salt and pepper, to taste.

YIELD: 6 TO 8 SERVINGS

Sweet Italian Chicken-Sausage Patties

1 & 1/3 to 1 & 1/2 pounds ground **chicken breast**

3 cloves **garlic,** chopped

3 tablespoons chopped fresh flat-leaf **parsley**

1/4 cup grated **parmesan,** Parmigiano Reggiano, or Romano cheese

1 teaspoon **fennel** seeds

1 teaspoon freshly ground black **pepper** (1/3 of a palmful)

3/4 teaspoon **salt** (eyeball it)

2 tablespoons **extra-virgin olive oil** (evoo) (twice around the pan)

Mix chicken with garlic, parsley, cheese, fennel, pepper, and salt. Form 6 large, thin patties, 4 to 5 inches in diameter, or 12 small patties, 2 to 3

inches. Preheat a large, nonstick skillet over medium heat and fry patties
in evoo until done, 3 to 4 minutes on each side.

Birds in a Nest

See also Late-Night Bites for more Nesters

1/2 cup **extra-virgin olive oil** (evoo) (eyeball it)
1 large clove **garlic**, cracked from skin
6 thick slices crusty Italian **semolina bread**
6 extra-large **eggs**
1 small jar (6 ounces) **roasted red peppers**
Salt and freshly ground black **pepper**, to taste
1/2 cup grated **parmesan**, Parmigiano Reggiano, or Romano
      cheese

Preheat a 2-burner nonstick griddle or very large nonstick skillet over
medium heat.

Pour evoo into a small bowl or dish and add garlic. Microwave oil on high
for 30 seconds.

Using a small knife or just your fingers, cut out or pull away a small
amount of bread from the center of each slice. Brush garlic oil on bread
and arrange the pieces on the griddle. Crack each egg and drop it into its
"nest," or the hole in each slice of bread. Drain and slice red peppers. Add
a strip or two of red pepper to each nest. Season with salt and pepper
and sprinkle a little cheese into each nest. Tent the pan with aluminum foil
and let the eggs sit in their nests 5 minutes, then transfer them to a platter
and serve with chicken-sausage patties.

YIELD: 6 SERVINGS

MENU ANYTIME SPRINGTIME BRUNCH

~ PASTA FRITTATA

~ PEAS AND CARROTS SPRING SALAD

Pasta Frittata

Salt and freshly ground black **pepper,** to taste

1 box (12 ounces) egg **fettuccini**

2 tablespoons **extra-virgin olive oil** (evoo) (twice around the pan)

2 tablespoons **butter**

1 cup **heavy cream**

1 cup grated **Parmigiano** Reggiano cheese

1/4 to 1/2 teaspoon grated or ground **nutmeg** (eyeball it)

1/4 cup chopped fresh flat-leaf **parsley**

12 extra-large **eggs,** beaten

Preheat oven to 425°F.

Bring a large pot of water to a boil and salt it. Add pasta and cook to a chewy al dente, about 6 minutes; pasta will continue to cook in frittata. Drain and reserve.

Heat a large, nonstick, ovenproof skillet over medium-high heat. If you don't have an ovenproof skillet, cover handle tightly in aluminum foil to protect it. Add evoo and butter and let butter melt into evoo. Add cream and reduce for about 3 minutes. Add cheese, nutmeg, salt, and pepper. Toss sauce with cooked pasta to coat. Add parsley and beaten eggs to the skillet and stir gently to combine. Allow eggs to set on the bottom of the pan and become firm. Transfer pan to hot oven and bake until golden, about 10 minutes. Serve from the pan or transfer to a platter. Serve hot or cold, cutting frittata into wedges.

YIELD: 6 SERVINGS

Peas and Carrots Spring Salad

1 sack (12 ounces) mixed baby **greens** (available on produce aisle)

20 leaves fresh **basil,** shredded or torn

2 cups shredded **carrots** (available preshredded on produce aisle)

1 cup frozen baby **peas**

1 **shallot,** finely chopped

3 tablespoons distilled **white vinegar**

1/3 cup **extra-virgin olive oil** (evoo) (eyeball it)

Salt and freshly ground black **pepper,** to taste

Combine greens and basil on a platter. Top with shredded carrots and peas. Combine shallots and vinegar and let stand 5 to 10 minutes. Whisk evoo into vinegar to combine. Drizzle the dressing evenly over the salad and season with salt and pepper.

YIELD: 6 SERVINGS

MENU BRUNCH BETWEEN THE BREAD

~ SUPER-STUFFED MONTE CRISTO SANDWICHES

~ YOGURT CRUNCH

Super-Stuffed Monte Cristo Sandwiches

8 slices center-cut or applewood-smoked **bacon**

4 large **eggs**, beaten

1/4 cup **half-and-half**, warmed in microwave or on stove

1/4 teaspoon grated fresh **nutmeg** or ground (eyeball it)

1/2 teaspoon freshly ground black **pepper** (eyeball it)

2 tablespoons **butter**

8 thick slices soft whole-grain, white, or challah **bread**

1/2 cup brown **mustard**

1/2 cup whole-berry **cranberry sauce**

1/2 pound deli-sliced **Havarti** cheese

1 pound deli-sliced **ham**

1 pound deli-sliced **turkey breast**

1 & 1/2 cups medium to dark amber **maple syrup**

Heat a griddle pan or large skillet over medium-high heat. Cook bacon until done, 5 minutes, and remove to paper towels to drain. Drain off fat. Reheat griddle over medium heat.

Beat eggs with half-and-half, nutmeg, and pepper. Add 1 tablespoon butter to the griddle and let it melt. Turn 4 slices bread in egg batter then place on griddle. Turn bread after it browns, 2 to 3 minutes; spread mustard on 2 slices bread and top the other 2 slices with cranberry sauce. Place a slice of cheese on each slice. Add 2 slices bacon, ham, and turkey to bottoms then set tops in place and press sandwiches together. Turn the sandwiches a couple of times and let set a minute or 2 to melt cheese and warm meats. Repeat to make 2 more sandwiches. Cut sandwiches from corner to corner to serve.

Heat syrup in microwave-safe container for 30 seconds. Drizzle syrup over sandwiches at the table or serve syrup in small ramekins for dipping.

YIELD: 4 SERVING

Yogurt Crunch

6 cups vanilla **yogurt**
4 firm granola bars, any flavor
1/2 cup chopped **walnuts,** pecans, or hazelnuts

Pour yogurt into a bowl. Place granola bars in a plastic food storage bag and crush; add to yogurt along with nuts. Stir to combine all ingredients and transfer to cups to serve.

YIELD: 4 SERVINGS

MENU **ACCESSIBLE ELEGANCE**

~ **CRAB-STUFFED PORTOBELLOS AND CITRUS-MUSTARD DRESSED GREENS**

~ **TINY TRIFLES**

Crab-Stuffed Portobellos and Citrus-Mustard Dressed Greens

1/4 cup **extra-virgin olive oil** (evoo) (eyeball it)

4 large portobello **mushroom caps**, wiped clean with damp cloth

Grill seasoning, such as Montreal Steak Seasoning by McCormick

3 tablespoons **butter**, softened

1 **bay leaf**

2 ribs **celery** from heart of stalk, chopped

1 small **onion**, chopped

1 small **red bell pepper**, seeded and chopped

Salt and freshly ground black **pepper**, to taste

2 teaspoons **Old Bay Seasoning** (a palmful) OR 1 teaspoon poultry seasoning plus 1 teaspoon paprika

2 teaspoons **hot sauce**, such as Tabasco (eyeball it)

6 ounces lump **crabmeat** (available in 6-ounce tubs in fresh seafood section)

3 slices white **bread**, toasted

1 cup **chicken broth**

A handful of chopped fresh flat-leaf **parsley**

SALAD

1 rounded tablespoon **lemon curd** (available in jars near jams and jellies)

2 tablespoons white wine **vinegar** (eyeball it)

2 teaspoons **Dijon** mustard

1/3 cup **extra-virgin olive oil** (evoo) (eyeball it)

Salt and freshly ground black **pepper**, to taste

1 sack (8 ounces) mixed baby **greens** (available on produce aisle)

Heat a grill pan or large nonstick skillet over medium-high heat. Pour evoo into a small dish. Using a pastry brush, coat mushroom caps with oil. Grill until tender, about 10 minutes, and season with grill seasoning blend.

Preheat a medium skillet over medium-high heat. Add remaining evoo (from brushing mushroom caps) to skillet and combine with 2 tablespoons butter. Let butter melt into oil and add bay leaf, celery, onion, and bell pepper; season with salt, pepper, and Old Bay Seasoning or poultry

seasoning and paprika and cook until almost tender, 3 to 5 minutes. Add hot sauce to vegetables. Run your fingers through the crab to make sure there are no pieces of shell in the meat. Break up crabmeat with fingertips and mix into veggies. Butter toasted bread with remaining tablespoon of butter; cut toast into small dice. Add toast to veggies and moisten stuffing with chicken broth. Adjust seasonings. Top cooked portobello caps with stuffing. Garnish with chopped parsley.

Make the salad dressing: In a small bowl, combine lemon curd with vinegar and mustard using a whisk. Whisk in evoo in a slow stream and season with salt and pepper. Pour lettuce into a bowl and drizzle dressing over the top. Serve mushroom caps with greens on the side.

YIELD: 4 SERVINGS

Tiny Trifles

4 individual (3-inch) **sponge cakes**

4 tablespoons orange or almond **liqueur**

1/2 cup seedless **raspberry all-fruit spread** or preserves

2 individual cups (4 ounces each) prepared **vanilla pudding** (available on dairy aisle)

1/4 cup sliced **almonds**

4 large **strawberries,** hulled and sliced

1 **kiwi,** peeled and diced

Douse cakes with liqueur. Spread with fruit spread. Top with a layer of vanilla pudding and sprinkle pudding with sliced almonds. Arrange berries and kiwi over the pudding and nuts.

YIELD: 4 SERVINGS

MENU CÔTE D'AZUR LUNCH

~ CRUDITÉS AND 3 SAUCES

~ HAM, COUNTRY PÂTÉ, AND CHEESE PLATTER

Crudités and 3 Sauces

ANCHOVY SAUCE

2 tins flat-fillet **anchovies**, lightly drained

1 tablespoon small **capers** in brine

2 tablespoons **caper brine**

1 clove **garlic**, cracked from skin

1/2 cup **extra-virgin olive oil** (evoo) (eyeball it)

BLACK OLIVE AND PARMIGIANO SAUCE

1/2 cup pitted niçoise or Kalamata **olives**

2 tablespoons red wine **vinegar** (eyeball it)

1 teaspoon dried **thyme** or 2 tablespoons fresh thyme leaves

1/3 cup **extra-virgin olive oil** (evoo) (eyeball it)

1/4 cup grated **Parmigiano** Reggiano cheese (a handful)

GARDEN TOMATO AND SCALLION SAUCE

2 plum **tomatoes**, seeded and chopped

2 **scallions**, whites and tops, thinly sliced

2 tablespoons chopped fresh flat-leaf **parsley** (a palmful)

Extra-virgin olive oil (evoo), for drizzling

Coarse **salt** and freshly ground black **pepper**, to taste

CRUDITÉS

2 large **eggs**

1 seedless **cucumber**, halved across then quartered lengthwise

1 head **celery**, trimmed, separated, and wiped clean, ribs left whole

4 **scallions**, whole, cleaned and roots trimmed

4 large **radishes**, cleaned but left whole with greens intact

4 baby **zucchini**, washed

4 small **carrots**, peeled and left whole

2 vine-ripened **tomatoes**

Make the anchovy sauce: Place anchovies, capers, caper brine, and garlic in a food processor or blender and turn the machine on. Stream in evoo to form a thick dressing. Scrape the dressing into a small serving cup or bowl. Clean the processor bowl or the blender and return it to its base.

Make the black olive and Parmigiano sauce: Place olives, vinegar, and thyme in processor or blender. Turn machine on and stream in evoo. When dressing forms, stop machine and add cheese. Pulse-process cheese into dressing then transfer dressing into a second cup or small bowl.

Make the garden tomato and scallion sauce: In a small mixing bowl, combine tomatoes, scallions, and parsley. Drizzle the sauce with evoo and season it with salt and pepper, to taste.

Prepare the crudités: Place eggs in a small pot. Cover eggs with water and bring water to a boil. Cover pot and remove from heat. Let eggs stand 10 minutes. Drain eggs then crack shells by rattling cooked eggs inside empty, covered pot. Peel and cool eggs under cold running water.

Arrange the vegetables in a flowerpot, building high and stuffing the pot tightly. Nest whole eggs and whole tomatoes among the vegetables. Serve your vegetable masterpiece with sauces to pass at table.

INSIDE·SCOOP

I have been in love with the French Riviera since I saw "To Catch a Thief" as a girl. Finally, at 35, I had the great fortune to visit the area in living color, and it was more spectacular than I imagined. My favorite lunch, a habit by week's end, was crudités and some cheese and bread (washed down with a crisp rosé, of course). The crudités at many restaurants were edible works of art, still lifes of whole, perfect, freshly picked vegetables served with three sauces for dipping and topping. And the cheese—well, as they say, when in France. . .! For fun, serve the crudités in a 6- or 7-inch plain terra cotta flowerpot. It looks awesome, is reusable, and it'll only cost you a few bucks at any garden shop.

Ham, Country Pâté, and Cheese Platter

2 logs or disks **goat cheese** (3-4 ounces each), fresh or aged, plain or with ash or herbs

1 small wheel (4 inches) **Camembert**, Liverot, or Pont l'Evêque cheese (available in specialty cheese case)

1/3 pound **Gruyère** or Comte cheese

1 slice (1/2 pound) country-style pork liver **pâté**

1 jar **cornichons** or baby gherkin pickles, drained

Stone-ground **mustard**

1/2 pound mild, cooked **ham** or prosciutto cotto

1 package thin **bread sticks**

1/2 pound seedless red **grapes**, broken into small bunches

1 baguette, sliced

Arrange cheeses and pâté on a cutting board or platter. Place cornichons and mustard in ramekins and add to board or platter. Wrap a slice of ham around each of several bread sticks and add to platter. Tuck grapes in among cheeses and ham-wrapped bread sticks. Arrange bread on the platter, along with soft-cheese spreaders and a cheese knife, and serve by passing at the table.

YIELD: 4 SERVINGS

MENU **CINQUE TERRA LUNCH**

~ **POTATOES WITH ANCHOVY AND ROSEMARY**

~ **MIXED GREENS WITH BALSAMIC VINEGAR AND STRAWBERRIES**

Potatoes with Anchovy and Rosemary

1/4 cup **extra-virgin olive oil** (evoo), for drizzling

3 small white oval **potatoes** or 4 fat fingerling potatoes, thinly sliced (1/8- to 1/4-inch thick) lengthwise (16 slices total)

Salt and freshly ground black **pepper**, to taste

6 stems **rosemary**, leaves chopped (5–6 tablespoons)

32 flat **anchovy fillets**

3 small ripe plum **tomatoes**, seeded and chopped

Crusty **bread**, to pass at table

Preheat oven to 425°F.

Drizzle the evoo onto a cookie sheet with an edge or in a shallow roasting pan. Coat potato slices in evoo and season lightly with salt and more liberally with pepper. Arrange a bed of chopped rosemary on top of each potato slice. Set 2 anchovy fillets on each potato slice then scatter a few pieces of chopped tomato on top. Roast until potatoes are just tender, 12 to 15 minutes. Serve 4 slices per person.

YIELD: 4 SERVINGS

Cinque terra translates to "five lands" and refers to a string of five tiny villages near the Ligurian coast of Italy. To get there, go by train or boat; by car, it is many hours on less-than-perfect, winding mountain roads. The terraced cliffs that surround the tiny villages are a popular hiking destination, as the trails connecting the Cinque Terra wander through vineyards clinging to the cliffs. It is known among Italians as the poor man's Riviera. Me, rich or poor, I do not trek so well, especially in the heat: Eating and drinking are my preferred summer activities—pretty much the same as my winter activities. I decided to boat in with my sweetie and our friend Roberto. We had this fantastic lunch, which anyone can make, as the recipe calls for only a few inexpensive ingredients. I recommend a crisp, chilled Italian white wine, preferably from the Cinque Terra region, with this menu.

Mixed Greens with Balsamic Vinegar and Strawberries

This combination of thick, sweet vinegar and strawberries dates all the way back to Columbus. Traditionally, the combination is allowed to macerate and mature and is then served with roast pork. Fresh basil is added at the table.

In Cinque Terra, I discovered that sweet, freshly sliced berries were indeed refreshing against the sweet acidity of balsamic vinegar. I've also added basil directly to this salad.

2 hearts **romaine** lettuce, chopped

1 head **radicchio**, shredded

1 cup fresh **basil** tops, torn or shredded

1/2 pint **strawberries**, thinly sliced

3 tablespoons aged **balsamic vinegar**, 6 years or older, if available

1/4 cup **extra-virgin olive oil** (evoo) (eyeball it)

Salt and freshly ground black **pepper**, to taste

Combine romaine, radicchio, basil, and strawberries. Dress salad with vinegar, then evoo. Season with salt and pepper.

YIELD: 4 SERVINGS

TV DINNERS & SNACKS
7:00 - MIDNIGHT

*Bacon-Wrapped
Shrimp and Scallops
and Chinese-Barbecued-Chicken
Lettuce Wraps*

RECIPES ON PAGE 172

*Devilish Chili-Cheese Dogs and
Summer-ish Succotash Salad*

RECIPES ON PAGE 90

Long Live the Chicken à la King!

RECIPE ON PAGE 96

BISTRO MEALS

9:00 - MIDNIGHT

French Onion Tartlets

RECIPE ON PAGE 196

*Crispy Duck Salad with
Bitter Orange Vinaigrette*

RECIPE ON PAGE 197

11:00 - 4:00

Super Eggplant Subs

RECIPE ON PAGE 73

Green Ranch-Hand Eggs

RECIPE ON PAGE 228

Birds in a Nest

RECIPE ON PAGE 53

I'LL HAVE THE SALAD

~ SMOKED TURKEY WALDORF SALAD

~ CURRIED CASHEW-CHICKEN SALAD

Smoked Turkey Waldorf Salad

3 tablespoons **honey**

1 tablespoon **salt**

1/2 teaspoon **cayenne** pepper

2 tablespoons turbinado **sugar**

8 ounces **walnut halves** or pieces

2 heads **endive,** chopped

1 cup packed **watercress** leaves

1 & 1/2 pounds thick-cut **smoked turkey** from deli, cut into 1/2-inch-thick slices

1 green **apple,** such as Granny Smith, cored and chopped

1/2 pound seedless red **grapes,** stemmed and halved

1/4 **lemon**

1/4 cup **whipping cream**

1/4 cup **mayonnaise** or ranch dressing

Salt and freshly ground black **pepper,** to taste

Preheat oven to 425°F.

Combine honey, salt, cayenne, and sugar. Coat nuts in mixture and spread out on a cookie sheet. Roast nuts 3 or 4 minutes; remove and let cool.

Place endive, watercress, turkey, apple, and grapes in a large bowl. Squeeze a little lemon juice over the bowl and toss.

With an electric hand-mixer, whip cream to soft peaks; fold in mayo or ranch dressing. Add mixture to salad and toss to coat. Season with salt and pepper. Distribute among 4 plates and top with cooled caramelized nuts

YIELD: 4 SERVINGS

Curried Cashew-Chicken Salad

1 rotisserie chicken

1 cup **pea shoots** or spicy sprouts

1 cup shredded **carrots** (preshredded is available in the produce section)

4 **scallions**, sliced on an angle

1 can (6–8 ounces) sliced **water chestnuts** , drained

2 tablespoons mild **curry paste**

1/4 cup mango **chutney** or duck sauce

1/4 cup golden **raisins** (a healthy handful)

1 cup plain **yogurt**

Grated zest and juice of 1 **lime**

Salt and freshly ground black **pepper**, to taste

1/4 cup sunflower or peanut **oil**

3 inches fresh **gingerroot**, peeled and cut into long matchsticks

1 sack (12 ounces) baby **greens**

1 cup unsalted roasted **cashews**

Remove skin from chicken; discard. Remove meat. Dice meat and add to a large mixing bowl. Add pea shoots, carrots, scallions, water chestnuts, curry, chutney, raisins, yogurt, lime zest, and lime juice. Mix thoroughly to combine and evenly coat the salad. Season with salt and pepper.

Heat oil in a small skillet over medium heat. Add ginger and fry until crisp, 2 to 3 minutes; drain.

Arrange greens on 4 large plates and arrange chicken salad on greens. Top with cashews and some fried ginger, then serve.

YIELD: 4 SERVINGS

MENU **USER-FRIENDLY LUNCHEON**

~ **ROSEMARY AND HAM SCONES**

~ **SALMON CAKES SALAD**

Rosemary and Ham Scones

As a close second choice, you can serve warm, buttered pumpernickel bread with the salmon cakes salad instead of these scones.

1 box Jiffy brand **biscuit mix**

4 small stems **rosemary**, leaves picked and finely chopped (3 tablespoons)

1/2 cup **heavy cream**

A couple pinches of **salt**

3 pieces deli-sliced glazed **smoked ham**, chopped (about 1/8 pound)

1 tablespoon grated **orange** zest

2 teaspoons **sugar**

Preheat oven to 375°F.

Mix together biscuit mix, rosemary, cream, salt, ham, and orange zest. Pile mixture into 4 large mounds or 8 small mounds onto a nonstick cookie sheet. Sprinkle with a little sugar and bake until light golden brown, 10 to 12 minutes for large scones, 7 to 8 minutes for small scones. If you're making salmon cakes salad (recipe follows), leave the oven on.

YIELD: 4 SERVINGS

Salmon Cakes Salad

SALMON CAKES

2 cans (14 ounces each) **salmon** with bones, drained

2 **egg whites**, beaten

1/3 cup Italian **bread crumbs** (a couple of handfuls)

1 tablespoon **Old Bay seasoning**

A few drops of **hot sauce**, such as Tabasco

2 tablespoons chopped fresh flat-leaf **parsley**

3–4 tablespoons chopped **roasted red pepper**, from a jar, drained

Salt and freshly ground black **pepper**, to taste

1 tablespoon vegetable **oil** (once around the pan)

SALAD

1 head **frisée** lettuce, coarsely chopped

1 **endive**, sliced

1 **romaine** heart, chopped

2 cups baby **spinach** leaves (just over 1/4 pound) (available in bulk bins)

1 navel **orange**, peeled and chopped

1/2 small red **onion**, thinly sliced

1 tablespoon grated **orange zest**

3 tablespoons red wine **vinegar**

1/4 to 1/3 cup **extra-virgin olive oil**, (evoo) (eyeball it)

Salt and freshly ground black **pepper**, to taste

Preheat the oven to 375°F.

Make the salmon cakes: Heat a medium ovenproof skillet over medium-high heat (if you don't have an ovenproof skillet, wrap the handle tightly in aluminum foil). Combine salmon, egg whites, bread crumbs, Old Bay, Tabasco, parsley, roasted red pepper, salt, and pepper. Form mixture into 4 patties, 1-inch thick. Pour vegetable oil into hot pan. Add patties and cook a minute or 2 on each side, then transfer to oven and bake for about 8 minutes.

Make the salad: Combine frisée, endive, romaine, spinach, chopped orange, and red onion in a salad bowl. Combine orange zest and vinegar in a small bowl. Whisk in evoo to desired bite and consistency. Dress and toss salad. Season with salt and pepper. Divide among 4 plates. Top salads with warm salmon cakes and serve with ham and rosemary scones.

YIELD: 4 SERVINGS

WRAPS "TO GO"

Shrimp or Chicken Caesar Romaine Lettuce Wraps

This recipe requires no cooking, is served cold, and travels well, so it makes a perfect picnic selection in the hot summer months as well. If you think that you don't like anchovies, try them in this sauce. They just taste salty and yummy!

2 hearts **romaine** lettuce

1 pound fully cooked jumbo **shrimp** (available at the seafood counter)

1 **rotisserie chicken**

4 heaping tablespoons reduced-fat **mayonnaise**

1 clove **garlic,** crushed

Grated zest and juice of 1 **lemon**

2 tablespoons **anchovy paste** (optional)

1/2 cup grated **parmesan** or Parmigiano Reggiano cheese

2 teaspoons **Worcestershire** sauce (eyeball it)

1 teaspoon freshly ground black **pepper** (eyeball it)

3 tablespoons **extra-virgin olive oil** (evoo) (three times around the pan)

Cut bottoms off the romaine and cut the heads in half lengthwise. Wash lettuce and separate the leaves. Let lettuce dry in the dish rack while you prepare the rest of the menu.

Remove the tails from the shrimp and place shrimp in a bowl, or pack for travel, if this is a picnic meal. Remove the chicken meat from the chicken. Slice the meat up on an angle. Arrange on a plate or in a plastic container.

Place mayo, garlic, lemon zest, lemon juice, anchovy paste, cheese, Worcestershire, and pepper in a food processor or blender and turn it on. Stream in the evoo through the center of the lid. When the dressing is combined, remove it with a spatula to a bowl or plastic container.

Place lettuce on a serving platter or pack in large plastic bag or container to travel. Place lettuce, shrimp, chicken, and dressing on the table, and let everyone build their own wraps: To assemble, spread dressing onto a lettuce leaf. Fill leaf with a large shrimp or sliced cold chicken, like a lettuce taco, and eat.

YIELD: 4 SERVINGS

MENU **BEACH BODY LUNCH IN 30**

~ FRUIT SOUP
~ BEEF AND BROCCOLI SALAD

Fruit Soup

Have this refreshing and cool treat as a starter or a dessert to your salad meal.

1 large, ripe **cantaloupe**, peeled, seeded, and cut into chunks
2 cans (6 ounces each) **pineapple juice**
Juice of 1 **lime**
2 **kiwis**, peeled and chopped

Combine cantaloupe, pineapple juice, and lime juice in a food processor and process until smooth. Pour soup into shallow bowls or cups and top with chopped kiwi.

YIELD: 4 SERVINGS

Beef and Broccoli Salad

SALAD

4 **beef tenderloin steaks** (6 ounces each) (1-inch thick)

Salt and freshly ground black **pepper**

Vegetable-oil **cooking spray**

1 large head **broccoli**, stem trimmed and cut into florets

1 sack (6-8 ounces) mixed baby **greens**

1 **red bell pepper**, seeded and very thinly sliced

4 **scallions**, sliced on an angle into 1-inch pieces

1 cup **pea pods**, sliced on an angle

1 cup shredded **carrots** (preshredded is available in sacks on the produce aisle)

8 **hot cherry peppers** or pepperoncini, chopped

2 tablespoons chopped fresh **cilantro** (optional)

DRESSING

1/4 cup **duck sauce** or sweet and sour sauce

1 inch fresh **gingerroot**, peeled and finely chopped

Juice of 1 **lime**

2 tablespoons **rice wine vinegar** or white vinegar

1/2 to 1 teaspoon crushed **red pepper flakes**

1/4 cup vegetable **oil**

Make the salad: Preheat a grill pan over high heat. Season steak with salt and pepper. Spray grill pan with cooking spray. Grill meat 3 to 5 minutes per side for medium-rare to medium-well doneness. Remove meat and let stand 10 minutes.

In a pan, bring 1 inch of water to a bubble. Add a pinch of salt, then broccoli. Steam until broccoli is cooked, but still firm, 3 to 5 minutes. Drain in colander and run cold water over it to cool.

Arrange greens and broccoli on large platter or individual dinner plates. Arrange bell peppers, scallions, pea pods, carrots, cherry peppers, and cilantro on greens.

Make the dressing: Combine duck or sweet and sour sauce with ginger, lime juice, vinegar, and crushed red pepper flakes. Whisk in oil.

Slice steaks and arrange on salad; drizzle with dressing. Season the salad with additional salt and pepper.

YIELD: 4 SERVINGS

MENU BETWEEN-THE-BREAD MEALS— NOW THAT'S A SANDWICH!

~ SPINACH-ARTICHOKE PASTA SALAD

~ SUPER EGGPLANT SUBS

Spinach-Artichoke Pasta Salad

Salt and freshly ground black **pepper,** to taste

1 package (12–16 ounces) fresh mushroom-, chicken prosciutto-, or spinach-filled **tortellini,** such as Contadina or Buitoni brands

A handful of **sun-dried tomatoes,** coarsely chopped

1/2 pound fresh baby **spinach**

1 can (15 ounces) baby **artichoke hearts** in water, drained and chopped

1 **roasted red pepper** from a jar, drained and chopped

1/2 small red **onion,** chopped

1 clove **garlic,** cracked from skin

Grated zest of 1 **lemon**

2 teaspoons **lemon juice** (eyeball it)

2 tablespoons red wine **vinegar** (a couple of splashes)

1/4 cup **extra-virgin olive oil** (evoo)

1 tablespoon fresh **thyme,** chopped, or 1/2 teaspoon dried leaves (eyeball it)

Bring 5 or 6 inches of water to a boil in a large pot. Salt boiling water and add tortellini. Cook 2 minutes, then add sun-dried tomatoes. Cook tortellini until it is just tender and floating, another 2 to 3 minutes. Drain tortellini and tomatoes, then cool by spreading them out on a large plate or cookie sheet in a single layer.

Coarsely chop spinach. In a large bowl, combine spinach with artichokes, roasted red pepper, and red onion.

Chop garlic, then add 1/2 teaspoon of salt and mash it into a paste with the flat of your knife. Transfer garlic paste to a small bowl and add lemon zest, lemon juice, and vinegar. Whisk in evoo, thyme, and pepper. Add pasta and sun-dried tomatoes to the spinach salad. Dress salad and gently toss. Serve or refrigerate until needed.

YIELD: 4 SERVINGS

Super Eggplant Subs

1 cup **extra-virgin olive oil** (evoo)

2 large cloves **garlic**, cracked from skins, plus 2 cloves garlic, chopped

2 medium, firm **eggplants**

Salt and freshly ground black **pepper**, to taste

1/2 red **onion**, chopped

1 can (28 ounces) chopped **fire-roasted tomatoes**, such as Muir Glen brand

1 small can (8 ounces) **tomato sauce**

4 **sub rolls**, split

1 cup fresh **basil** leaves, thinly sliced or torn

1/2 cup grated **Parmigiano** Reggiano cheese

1 pound **smoked mozzarella**, thinly sliced

Preheat oven to 450°F.

Heat a small skillet with evoo and cracked garlic in it over medium-low heat. Meanwhile, trim ends off eggplants and remove a sliver off one side, so the eggplant sits flat while you slice it. Cut eggplant into 1/2-inch-thick slices. Arrange eggplant slices on cookie sheets. When garlic sizzles in oil, use a pastry brush to brush both sides of sliced eggplant with garlic oil. Season eggplant with salt and pepper and roast until tender, about 15 minutes, turning once.

Meanwhile, place 2 tablespoons of the remaining garlic oil in a medium skillet over medium-high heat. To hot oil add chopped garlic and red onions. Sauté onions and garlic 2 to 3 minutes, then add tomatoes and tomato sauce; season with salt and pepper. Lower heat and allow sauce to thicken.

Remove eggplant from the oven. Arrange open sub rolls on a broiler pan. Preheat broiler. Pile layers of eggplant, roasted tomato sauce, and basil into sub rolls, equally dividing ingredients among the rolls. Top subs with Parmigiano and smoked mozzarella cheeses. Place under broiler to melt cheese. Serve hot.

YIELD: 4 SANDWICHES

BURGERS WITH STYLE

~ SEAFOOD BURGERS

~ CUBANO BURGERS WITH MANGO–BLACK BEAN SALSA

Seafood Burgers

SEAFOOD BURGERS

1/2 pound raw small salad **shrimp** (300 count to the pound)

6 ounces (drained weight) lump **crabmeat**

1 small rib **celery**, from the heart, with greens, finely chopped

3 **scallions**, finely chopped

1/2 small **red bell pepper**, finely chopped

1 clove **garlic**, minced

A handful of fresh flat-leaf **parsley** leaves, chopped

1 tablespoon **Old Bay seasoning**

1/2 teaspoon **cayenne** pepper

1 teaspoon **chili powder**

Zest of 1 **lemon**

Salt and freshly ground black **pepper**

2 tablespoons **extra-virgin olive oil** (evoo) (twice around the pan)

4 plain or sourdough sandwich-size **English muffins**, such as Thomas's brand

Butter, for spreading

Lemon wedges, for squeezing

4 leaves Boston **lettuce** or leaf lettuce

1/2 cup spicy **cocktail sauce**

Grind shrimp into a paste in food processor and transfer to a bowl using a rubber spatula. Add crabmeat to the bowl, breaking it up and flaking it as you add it. Add celery, scallions, red bell peppers, garlic, parsley, Old Bay, cayenne, chili powder, lemon zest, salt, and pepper. Stir to combine.

Preheat a large nonstick skillet over medium-high heat. Add evoo. Using a large metal scoop or spoon, scoop 4 mounds of seafood mixture into the pan. Gently pat down to form patties and fry until the shrimp turns whitish pink and the patties are evenly golden, 3 to 5 minutes on each side.

Split and toast the English muffins. Butter the muffin bottoms. Place burgers on muffin bottoms and squeeze lemon juice over them, then top with lettuce. Slather the top of the muffins with cocktail sauce and set in place; serve.

YIELD: 4 BURGERS

Cubano Burgers with Mango–Black Bean Salsa

BURGERS

1 package (1 & 1/3 pounds) ground **turkey breast**

1/3 pound deli-sliced **smoked ham**, chopped

2 cloves **garlic**, minced

1/4 **red bell pepper**, finely chopped

3 **scallions**, finely chopped

2 tablespoons chopped fresh **cilantro**

1 tablespoon **grill seasoning**, such as Montreal Grill Seasoning for Steak by McCormick

Vegetable **oil** or olive oil, for drizzling

8 deli slices (1/3 pound) **Swiss cheese**

4 Portuguese **rolls** or crusty Kaiser rolls, split

2 large dill **pickles**, thinly sliced lengthwise

Sliced **banana pepper rings**, drained

Yellow **mustard**

1 sack (12 ounces) **plantain chips**, such as Goya brand (available on international food aisle)

SALSA

1 jar (16 ounces) **black bean salsa**

1 ripe **mango**, peeled and diced

2 tablespoons chopped fresh **cilantro**

1/4 **red bell pepper**, finely chopped

Make the burgers: Place turkey in a mixing bowl and add ham, garlic, red bell pepper, scallions, cilantro, and grill seasoning; combine. Form mixture into 4 large patties; drizzle patties with oil.

Heat a large nonstick skillet over medium-high heat. Cook patties until done, 5 to 6 minutes on each side, topping each patty with 2 slices Swiss cheese in the last 2 minutes of cooking time.

Place burgers on bun bottoms and top with sliced dill pickles and banana peppers. Transfer salsa to a serving bowl and top with mango, cilantro, and red bell pepper. Slather the bun tops with mustard and set in place. Serve burgers with plantain chips, and pass salsa for dipping chips or to top burgers.

YIELD: 4 SERVINGS

MENU **URBAN COWBOY**

~ **URBAN COWBOY TURKEY BURGERS**

~ **SPICY "O-NUTS"**

Urban Cowboy Turkey Burgers

8 slices turkey **bacon** or turkey bacon with black pepper or applewood-smoked bacon

1 package (1 & 1/3 pounds) ground **turkey breast**

2 cloves **garlic**, finely chopped

1 large **shallot** or 1/4 red onion, finely chopped

2 tablespoons chopped fresh **thyme** or 1 teaspoon dried thyme

2 tablespoons chopped fresh **cilantro** (parsley may be substituted)

1/2 small green, red, or yellow **bell pepper**, seeded and finely chopped

1 serrano or **jalapeño pepper**, seeded and finely chopped

2 teaspoons ground **cumin**

1–2 teaspoons **hot sauce**, such as Tabasco (eyeball it)

2 teaspoons Montreal Steak Seasoning by McCormick or other **grill seasoning** blend

Vegetable **oil** or olive oil, for drizzling

1/2 pound deli-sliced **pepper-Jack cheese**

4 crusty Kaiser **rolls**, split

1 cup sweet **red pepper relish** (available on condiment aisle) (pepper jelly may be substituted)

Red leaf **lettuce**

Chop garlic and veggies.

Heat a large nonstick skillet over medium-high heat; cook bacon until crisp. Remove bacon, wipe excess grease from skillet, and return skillet to heat.

While bacon is cooking, combine turkey, garlic, shallot or onion, thyme, cilantro or parsley, bell pepper, serrano or jalapeño pepper, cumin, hot sauce, and grill seasoning. Divide mixture into 4 equal mounds then form into patties. Drizzle patties with vegetable oil to coat. Cook in skillet over medium-high heat until done, 5 to 6 minutes on each side, placing sliced cheese over the patties in the last 2 minutes of cooking.

Place cooked cheeseburgers on buns. Spread sweet relish on bun tops and set lettuce into place using relish as "glue." Top cheeseburgers with 2 slices bacon, then serve.

YIELD: 4 SERVINGS

Spicy "O-nuts"

Vegetable **oil**, for frying

1 extra-large sweet **onion**, peeled and separated into 3/4-inch-thick rings

2 cups complete **pancake mix**

1 bottle (12 ounces) **beer**

1 teaspoon sweet **paprika**

2 teaspoons **chili powder**

1 tablespoon **hot sauce**, such as Tabasco

Salt, to taste

Pour 1 inch vegetable oil into a large skillet over medium-high heat. To test the oil, add a 1-inch cube of bread to hot oil; if it turns deep golden brown in color in a count to 40, the oil is ready.

Place 1/4 cup pancake mix in a resealable bag and add onion rings. Toss to coat onion rings.

Mix together the remaining 1 & 3/4 cups pancake mix, beer, paprika, chili powder, and hot sauce. Working in batches of 5 to 6 slices, coat onion rings in batter and fry until evenly golden brown, 4 to 5 minutes. Transfer to paper towels to drain. Season o-nuts with salt while hot. Repeat with remaining onions. When all the onions are dipped and fried, turn off oil to cool before discarding. Serve o-nuts hot.

YIELD: 4 SERVINGS

INSIDE SCOOP

I was out in Park City, Utah, with friends, and we went to Zoom, Robert Redford's restaurant. We all loved the buffalo-style onion rings. My friend Jeff said the batter was so thick and puffy that the onion rings looked like glazed doughnuts. At home I use pancake batter to make a sweet batter for the rings, adding chili powder and cayenne to spice them up. Around the house, I call these "Jeff's Spicy O-nuts" because they always make me think of him. This meal is great served with a tossed salad and tortilla chlps.

WHEN JUST A SAMMY WILL DO— STAND-ALONE SANDWICHES

~ PORTUGUESE BRUNCHWICH

~ HORSERADISH AND BEEF BAGUETTES

~ BOMBAY BRUNCH WRAP

~ RACHAEL'S RACHELS

~ COBB SANDWICHES

~ DEVILED EGG SALAD ON PUMPERNICKEL

~ NEW ENGLAND TASTY TUNA MELT

Portuguese Brunchwich

2 tablespoons **extra-virgin olive oil** (evoo) (twice around the pan)

1/2 pound **chorizo** or linguiça sausage, chopped

2 cloves **garlic**, finely chopped

1 cup **canned diced tomatoes**, drained well

2 cups baby **spinach** leaves

8 large **eggs**, lightly beaten

Salt and freshly ground black **pepper**, to taste

4 Portuguese **rolls**, split

Heat a medium nonstick skillet over medium-high heat. Add evoo and sausage. Brown and sear sausage a minute, then add garlic and toss 30 seconds. Add tomatoes and spinach and toss to coat and cook another 2 minutes. Add eggs and scramble. Season with salt and pepper and pile the scramble of meat, veggies, and eggs onto the rolls. Serve hot.

YIELD: 4 SERVINGS

Horseradish and Beef Baguettes

4 lengths (6 inches each) crusty **baguette**

4 tablespoons prepared **horseradish**

2/3 cup **heavy cream**

2 tablespoons chopped **chives**

Salt and freshly ground black **pepper**, to taste

1/2 cup baby **spinach** leaves (a generous handful)

1/2 cup **arugula** or watercress leaves

4 **radishes**, thinly sliced

1 & 1/2 pounds deli-sliced **roast beef**

Split baguettes open. Combine horseradish, cream, and chives. Season the dressing with salt and pepper. Spread the dressing on bread. Fill the baguettes with a mixture of spinach and arugula leaves, sliced radishes, and beef.

YIELD: 4 SERVINGS

Bombay Brunch Wrap

In India, these wraps are called Frankies.

2 tablespoons vegetable **oil** or peanut oil (twice around the pan)
6 white **mushrooms**, sliced
1/2 small **red bell pepper**, chopped
3 **scallions**, chopped
1/4 cup diced canned **chiles**, drained
1 tablespoon mild to medium **curry paste**
8 large **eggs**
Salt
4 plain or spinach flour **tortillas**
1 cup mango **chutney**

Heat a nonstick skillet over medium-high heat. Add oil, then mushrooms, bell pepper, scallions, and chiles. Cook for 2 or 3 minutes, tossing and turning the veggies to sear at edges. Add curry paste to vegetables and work through. Beat eggs with a little salt and add to the pan. Scramble eggs with curried veggies and cook to desired consistency.

To soften and blister the tortillas, heat them for 30 seconds over open flame on burner or in a second skillet preheated over high heat for 30 seconds on each side. Spread chutney on tortillas and wrap and roll the eggs in them like a burrito.

YIELD: 4 SERVINGS

Rachael's Rachels

A Rachel is a pastrami Reuben. I make mine with turkey pastrami and a mixture of sweet red pepper relish and sauerkraut.

1 & 1/2 cups (about 1/2 pound) **sauerkraut**, drained
1/2 cup sweet **red pepper relish**
2 **scallions**, chopped
8 slices **pumpernickel bread** or marble rye
Spicy brown deli **mustard**
1/2 pound thinly sliced **Swiss cheese**
1 & 1/2 pounds **turkey pastrami**
2 tablespoons **butter**, cut into pats
4 half-sour, garlic, or dill **pickles**
Flavored **gourmet chips,** such as Terra Blue potato chips or Cape Cod Firecracker Barbecue chips

Combine sauerkraut, red pepper relish, and scallions. Set 4 slices bread on a work surface; spread with mustard. Build sandwiches: Layer on a couple of slices of Swiss, a pile of turkey pastrami, a mound of sauerkraut mixture, more cheese. Spread tops with mustard and set into place.

Heat a large nonstick skillet over medium heat and add a couple pats of butter. When butter melts, add sandwiches. Place a heavy pot lid into the skillet to help press sandwiches as they grill. A second small skillet may also be used and weighted down with heavy cans.

Grill sandwiches 3 or 4 minutes per side, and serve with pickles and chips.

YIELD: 4 SERVINGS

Cobb Sandwiches

8 slices applewood-smoked **bacon**
4 sandwich-size sourdough **English muffins**
1/3 pound **blue cheese** crumbles
1 & 1/4 cups **ranch dressing**
2 **scallions**, chopped
Salt and freshly ground black **pepper,** to taste
1 & 1/2 pounds deli-sliced **chicken breast** or honey roast turkey
1 **avocado**, pitted and sliced
2 teaspoons **lemon juice**
1 vine-ripened **tomato,** sliced
4 leaves **lettuce**

Preheat broiler or a skillet over medium-high heat. Place bacon on a slotted broiler pan or in skillet, and cook until crisp. Drain on paper towels.

Lightly toast English muffins under broiler or in toaster oven.

Mix blue cheese, ranch dressing, and scallions. Add a few grinds of pepper to the dressing and spread muffin bottoms with half the dressing. Pile up the chicken or turkey on the dressing. To sliced avocado, add a few teaspoons lemon juice to slow browning. Arrange avocado and tomato slices on chicken or turkey and season with a pinch of salt. Set lettuce on top of tomatoes. Spread muffin tops with remaining dressing and set into place.

YIELD: 4 SERVINGS

Deviled Egg Salad on Pumpernickel

8 large **eggs**

1 teaspoon **paprika**

1 teaspoon **chili powder**

1 teaspoon **Worcestershire** sauce (eyeball it)

1 tablespoon **hot sauce,** such as Tabasco (eyeball it)

2 tablespoons prepared yellow **mustard**

3 tablespoons **mayonnaise** or ranch dressing

1/4 white **onion,** grated or minced

1 small rib **celery,** from the heart, with greens, finely chopped

2 tablespoons chopped **chives**

3 tablespoons green salad **olives** and **pimientos,** drained and finely chopped

Salt and freshly ground black **pepper,** to taste

8 slices **pumpernickel** bread

4 leaves **lettuce**

Place eggs in a pot and cover with water. Bring water to a boil. Cover the pot and turn off the heat; let eggs stand 10 minutes. Drain, then shake the eggs around in pot to crack the shells. Run eggs under cold water to peel and cool.

In a medium bowl combine paprika, chili powder, Worcestershire, hot sauce, mustard, mayo, onion and its juice, celery, chives, and olives. Coarsely chop eggs and add them to the bowl. Mix egg salad and season with salt and pepper. Lightly toast the bread and make sandwiches with mounds of deviled egg salad and lettuce.

YIELD: 4 SERVINGS

New England Tasty Tuna Melt

4 sandwich-size sourdough **English muffins**

2 large cans (9 ounces each) **tuna** in water, well-drained

5 rounded tablespoons sweet pickle **relish**

1/2 medium white **onion,** finely chopped

2 ribs **celery** with greens, finely chopped

2 teaspoons **Old Bay seasoning**

1/2 cup **mayonnaise** or ranch dressing

4 **radishes,** finely chopped

Salt and freshly ground black **pepper,** to taste

2 vine-ripened **tomatoes,** sliced

3/4 to 1 pound sharp **white cheddar** cheese, sliced

Preheat broiler. Place English muffins on a cookie sheet; lightly toast, then remove from oven. Leave the broiler on.

Mix tuna with relish, onion, celery, Old Bay, mayo, and radishes and combine well using 2 forks to mash the salad. Season with salt and pepper. Use a large scoop to mound salad evenly on top of the 8 muffin halves. Top each mound with tomato and cheese slices and place the open-faced sandwiches under the broiler to melt the cheese. Serve immediately.

YIELD: 4 SERVINGS

A COUPLE-A-CUP-O-SOUPS

~ **CRAB AND CORN CHOWDER CUP-O-SOUP**

~ **DOUBLE TOMATO AND PESTO CUP-O-SOUP**

~ **LEAN, MEAN, GREEN CUP-O-SOUP**

Crab and Corn Chowder Cup-o-Soup

2 tablespoons **butter**

2 slices thick-cut **bacon,** chopped

1 medium **onion,** chopped

1/2 **red bell pepper,** chopped

2 ribs **celery** with greens, chopped

4 sprigs fresh **thyme**

Salt and freshly ground black **pepper,** to taste

2 teaspoons **hot sauce,** such as Tabasco (eyeball it)

2 tablespoons all-purpose **flour**

2 teaspoons **Old Bay seasoning**

3 cups **half-and-half**

2 cups **chicken broth**

1 cup frozen **hash-brown potatoes** (available on dairy aisle)

6 ounces lump **crabmeat,** broken up

1 cup frozen **corn** kernels

2 sandwich-size **English muffins,** split

8 ounces extra-sharp **white cheddar** cheese, sliced

Chopped **chives** or fresh flat-leaf parsley, for garnish

In a medium pot over medium-high heat melt butter. Add bacon, onions, bell pepper, celery, and thyme. Season with salt, pepper, and hot sauce and cook 5 minutes. Stir in flour and Old Bay and cook a minute more.

Whisk in half-and-half, then add broth. Bring soup to a bubble, then stir in potatoes. Simmer until potatoes are cooked and soup has thickened to coat the back of a spoon, about 15 minutes. Add crabmeat and corn.

Heat toaster oven or broiler and toast English muffins. Top each muffin with cheese, return muffins to oven, and melt cheese.

Remove the thyme stems from the soup (the leaves will have fallen off into the soup). Stir and adjust seasonings. Pour soup into mugs. Garnish soup and muffins with chives or parsley. Serve soup with cheesy muffin for dipping.

YIELD: 4 SERVINGS

Double Tomato and Pesto Cup-o-Soup

Add chopped leftover meatloaf or meatballs, diced chicken, or bits of seafood to this soup to bump up the protein.

2 tablespoons **extra-virgin olive oil** (evoo) (twice around the pan)

1 clove **garlic**, chopped

2 **shallots**, finely chopped

1 **carrot**, peeled and finely chopped

1/2 cup loosely packed **sun-dried tomatoes**, chopped

Salt and freshly ground black **pepper**, to taste

1/2 cup dry **white wine** (eyeball it)

2–3 cups **chicken broth**

1 can (28 ounces) **concentrated crushed tomatoes**

1/2 cup store-bought **pesto sauce** (available in refrigerated section)

1 small brick **Asiago** or Parmigiano Reggiano cheese

Crusty **bread** or rolls, to pass at table

Heat a medium pot over medium heat. Add evoo, garlic, shallots, carrot, and sun-dried tomatoes. Season with salt and pepper and cook 5 minutes. Add wine and simmer it out, 2 minutes. Add 2 cups broth and the crushed tomatoes and heat to a bubble. Add up to 1 cup extra broth to bring soup to desired consistency. Stir in pesto. Adjust seasonings and pour soup into mugs. With a vegetable peeler, shave a few curls cheese over each mugful. Serve with bread for dipping.

YIELD: 4 SERVINGS

Lean, Mean, Green Cup-o-Soup

2 leeks, trimmed, halved lengthwise then sliced into 1/2-inch-thick half-moons

2 tablespoons extra-virgin olive oil (evoo) (twice around the pan)

1 medium zucchini, finely chopped

Salt and freshly ground black **pepper,** to taste

1 cup loosely packed fresh flat-leaf **parsley**

1 cup loosely packed **arugula** or watercress

1 cup loosely packed **basil** leaves

1/2 cup dry **white wine** (eyeball it)

1 quart vegetable stock

Crusty whole-grain **rolls,** for dipping

Rinse leeks thoroughly under running water or soak in a large bowl of cold water. Separate the layers to free any sandy grit. Drain the leeks well.

Heat a medium pot over medium heat. Add evoo, leeks, and zucchini; season with salt and pepper and sauté 5 or 6 minutes.

Grind up parsley, arugula or watercress, and basil in a food processor to a fine chop and add to the leeks and zucchini. Stir to combine. Add wine and let it evaporate and soak into the vegetables and greens, 1 minute or so. Add stock and raise soup to a boil. Reduce to a simmer over very low heat and cook 5 to 10 minutes. Serve the soup in mugs with bread for dipping.

YIELD: 4 SERVINGS

JUST A PERFECT FRENCH THING

Salade Niçoise à la Café 55

4 large **eggs**

1 & 1/2 pounds small red **potatoes**

Coarse **salt** and freshly ground black **pepper**, to taste

1 package (1 pound) trimmed fresh **green beans** or haricots verts

1 sack (12 ounces) mixed baby **greens**

1 **endive**, chopped

A handful of fresh flat-leaf **parsley** leaves

1 small **shallot**, minced

2 tablespoons white wine **vinegar**

Juice of 1/4 **lemon**

Crusty farmhouse-style whole-grain **bread**

1 rounded teaspoon **Dijon** mustard

3–4 tablespoons **extra-virgin olive oil** (evoo)

2 tins (6 ounces each) French or Italian **tuna** in olive oil

1/2 cup pitted niçoise **olives** (Kalamata may be substituted)

3 tablespoons drained **capers**

1 jar (4 ounces) or 2 (2-ounce) tins **anchovies**, drained (12 fillets)

Place eggs in a pot and cover them with cold water. Bring the water to a boil.

While the eggs come to a boil, place potatoes in a second pot, cover with water and bring to a boil. Salt the water and reduce heat to simmer.

When the eggs come to a boil, cover the pot and turn off the heat. Let the eggs sit 10 minutes, then run them under cold water, while still in the pot, to stop the cooking process. Drain them and knock them around in the pot with the lid on. Peel the cracked eggs and set aside.

When potatoes have cooked about 10 minutes, add green beans to the water and cook 3 minutes more. Lift beans out with a slotted spoon or a spider and transfer to cold-water bath to stop the cooking. Drain potatoes and return them to warm pot to dry them off. When cool enough to handle, quarter them.

Combine greens, endives, and parsley leaves in a salad bowl.

Start the vinaigrette: Place shallots, vinegar, and lemon juice in a small bowl and let stand 5 minutes.

Make the toast: Preheat broiler to high. Cut bread into thick slices and

toast, charring the edges, under broiler.

Add Dijon mustard to the vinaigrette. Whisk in evoo. Season with salt and pepper.

Chop beans and eggs into bite-size pieces. Open tuna and drain off excess oil.

Toss greens in vinaigrette. Add beans, eggs, potatoes, chunks of tuna, olives, capers, and anchovies to the top of the salad bowl and serve. Toss together at the table and pass with toast.

YIELD: 4 SERVINGS

INSIDE SCOOP

One afternoon I was flipping through a magazine and came across a picture of a personal hero: Bono. He was eating lunch in a straw cowboy hat, looking so perfectly relaxed that I felt a little intrusive just checking out the photo. The café looked like a commune built under beach tents of white canvas. When I recently traveled to St. Tropez, we drove three hours just to have lunch and check out the scene. In my memory, the café is a beach house, the back porch a sea of umbrellas under which droves of people flip-flop in from the white sand and blue water to feast on bread, vegetables, fish, and chilled rosé. I had a niçoise salad served in a small wooden bowl and several glasses of Domaine Ot rosé wine. This is my attempt at recreating the meal.

JUST A PERFECT ITALIAN THING

Ligurian Tuna Salad

4 thin-cut slices white **bread,** such as Pepperidge Farm brand

1/3 pound **green beans** or haricots verts, trimmed

Coarse **salt** and freshly ground black **pepper,** to taste

2 hearts **romaine** lettuce, trimmed and shredded

1 head **treviso** (long, purple, bitter lettuce) or radicchio, shredded

A handful of fresh **basil** leaves, torn

A handful of fresh flat-leaf **parsley** leaves, chopped

2 tins (6 ounces each) Italian **tuna** in oil, drained

1/2 cup large, green pitted Sicilian **olives**

1 cup canned **garbanzo beans,** drained

4 tablespoons **caper berries,** drained

12 bite-size **tomatoes** on the vine or grape tomatoes

1/2 cup frozen **corn**

Balsamic vinegar, 6 years or older, if available

Extra-virgin olive oil (evoo), for drizzling

Preheat broiler and lightly toast bread until very soft, 30 seconds on each side. While bread is warm, place 2 slices at a time on a rolling pin, molding them to the pin. Let bread cool—it will take a curled shape.

Place green beans in a small skillet and cover with water. Bring to a boil, add salt, and simmer 3 minutes. Drain beans and place in cold-water bath; drain again. Chop into bite-size pieces and reserve.

Arrange piles of chopped lettuce, treviso, basil, and parsley on 4 plates. Divide tuna, olives, garbanzo beans, green beans, caper berries, tomatoes, and corn among plates. Drizzle salads with balsamic vinegar and evoo. Season with salt and pepper and stand a curled toast up in the center of each plate, then serve.

YIELD: 4 SERVINGS

INSIDE SCOOP

I love traveling with my mama. Celebrating a banner
birthday year for her, we went to Portofino on the Ligurian
coast of Italy. One wonderful night, looking out over the starlit
Mediterranean, I looked over at her and was struck that she seemed
younger than me! She had a wash of pure wonderment that literally
made her glow. This is my way of remembering that special night.

Get supper on the table in no time flat
with these classic, casual, kid-friendly
meals. Perfect for busy families!

COOKING 'ROUND THE CLOCK

EARLY-BIRD
4 to 7
SPECIALS

RACHAEL RAY
30-MINUTE MEALS

MENU ENDLESS SUMMER

~ OIL-AND-VINEGAR SLAW

~ DEVILISH CHILI-CHEESE DOGS

~ SUMMER-ISH SUCCOTASH SALAD

Oil-and-Vinegar Slaw

2 tablespoons red wine **vinegar**

2 tablespoons **water**

1 tablespoon **sugar**

2 tablespoons peanut or vegetable **oil** (eyeball it)

1 sack (16 ounces) shredded **cabbage mix** for slaw salads (available on the produce aisle)

Salt and freshly ground black **pepper**, to taste

In a large bowl, mix vinegar, water, and sugar. Whisk in oil. Add cabbage to dressing and season with salt and pepper. Toss with fingers to combine. Adjust seasoning. Let stand 20 minutes. Retoss and serve.

YIELD: 6 TO 8 SERVINGS

Devilish Chili-Cheese Dogs

1 tablespoon **extra-virgin olive oil** (evoo) (once around the pan)

1 pound **ground sirloin**

Salt and freshly ground black **pepper**

2 teaspoons **Worcestershire** sauce (eyeball it)

1 small **onion**, chopped

2 cloves **garlic**, chopped

1 tablespoon **chili powder** (a palmful)

1 can (8 ounces) **tomato sauce**

8 fat or foot-long beef **franks**

1 tablespoon **butter**

1 tablespoon **hot sauce**, such as Tabasco

8 hot dog **buns**, toasted

2 cups (1 sack, 10 ounces) shredded **cheddar** cheese (preshredded is available on dairy aisle)

Heat a medium skillet over medium-high heat. Add evoo and meat and season with salt and pepper. Brown and crumble beef. Add Worcestershire, onion, garlic, and chili powder; cook together 5 minutes. Add tomato sauce and reduce heat to low.

Boil franks in a shallow skillet of water to warm through, 5 minutes. Drain and return pan to medium heat. Score casings on dogs. Melt butter in skillet and add hot sauce. Add dogs to skillet, browning and crisping the casings in hot sauce and butter.

Preheat broiler. Place devilish dogs in buns and top with chili and lots of cheese. Place devilish dogs under broiler and melt cheese. Serve immediately.

YIELD: 4 SERVINGS

Summer-ish Succotash Salad

2 cups frozen **corn** kernels, thawed
1 can (15 ounces) **butter beans**, drained
1 small **red bell pepper**, chopped
1/2 small red **onion**, chopped
1 tablespoon red wine **vinegar**
2 tablespoons chopped fresh flat-leaf **parsley** (a handful)
2 tablespoons peanut or vegetable **oil**
Salt and freshly ground black **pepper**, to taste

Combine corn, beans, bell pepper, and onion and toss with vinegar, parsley, oil, salt, and pepper.

YIELD: 4 SERVINGS

MENU AN ALL-AMERICAN SUPPER

~ PORK CHOPS WITH GOLDEN APPLESAUCE

~ CREAMY CORN

~ LEMON-SCENTED BROCCOLINI

Pork Chops with Golden Applesauce

4 golden delicious **apples**, chopped

1 teaspoon grated **lemon zest**

2 teaspoons fresh **lemon juice**

2 ounces golden **raisins** (a handful)

1 inch fresh **gingerroot**, peeled and grated

3 tablespoons light **brown sugar**

2 cups natural **apple juice** or cider

1/2 teaspoon **cinnamon**

1/4 teaspoon grated fresh **nutmeg**

2 tablespoons vegetable **oil** or olive oil (twice around the pan)

6 center-cut boneless **pork loin chops** (6–8 ounces each) (1-inch thick)

Salt and freshly ground black **pepper**

Make the applesauce: Combine apples, lemon zest, lemon juice, raisins, ginger, brown sugar, apple juice, cinnamon, and nutmeg in a medium pot over medium-high heat. Cook until a chunky sauce forms, 10 to 12 minutes, stirring occasionally. If sauce begins to spatter as it bubbles, reduce heat a little, but sauce should be allowed to reduce and form quickly. Once apples are soft and sauce forms, remove it from the heat.

Heat a large nonstick skillet over medium-high heat. Add oil to the pan. Season chops on one side with salt and pepper. Using a pair of tongs, add chops to hot oil, seasoned side down. Season the top side with salt and pepper, too. Brown and caramelize the chops 2 minutes on each side, then reduce heat to medium and cook until juices run clear, another 5 to 6 minutes, turning occasionally. Remove from heat and let chops rest a couple of minutes, allowing juices to redistribute. Top with generous portions of warm golden applesauce to serve.

YIELD: 6 SERVINGS

Creamy Corn

5 or 6 ears **corn** on the cob or 2 boxes (10 ounces each) frozen
   corn kernels, thawed

2 tablespoons **butter**

1 rib **celery** with greens, chopped

1/2 small **red bell pepper**, chopped

2 **scallions**, chopped

2 tablespoons fresh **thyme** leaves

Salt and freshly ground black **pepper**, to taste

1/2 cup **half-and-half**

Scrape corn kernels from cobs, if using.

Heat a medium skillet over medium heat. Add butter and let it melt; add
celery, bell pepper, and scallions and lightly sauté for 3 minutes, then add
corn and season with thyme, salt, and pepper. Cook 5 minutes, then add
half-and-half. Cover and cook over medium-low heat for 10 minutes.
Uncover and stir, then adjust seasonings.

YIELD: 6 SERVINGS

Lemon-Scented Broccolini

1 & 1/2 pounds **broccolini**

1 cup **water**

4 strips **lemon** peel

Salt, to taste

Place broccolini in a skillet. Add water and tuck lemon peels in and around
the broccolini. Cover and bring to a boil, then add a little salt. Keep
covered and cook broccolini until tender, 6 to 7 minutes. Drain and serve.

YIELD: 6 SERVINGS

MENU UK COMFORTS

~ 30-MINUTE SHEPHERD'S PIE

~ 5-MINUTE BREAD PUDDING

30-Minute Shepherd's Pie

2 pounds **potatoes**, such as russet, peeled and cubed

Salt and freshly ground black **pepper**

1 tablespoon **extra-virgin olive oil** (evoo) (once around the pan)

1 & 3/4 pounds **ground beef** or ground lamb

1 **carrot**, peeled and chopped

1 **onion**, chopped

2 tablespoons **butter**

2 tablespoons all-purpose **flour**

1 cup **beef stock** or broth

2 teaspoons **Worcestershire** sauce (eyeball it)

1/2 cup frozen **peas** (a couple of handfuls)

2 tablespoons **sour cream** or softened cream cheese

1 large **egg** yolk

1/2 cup **cream** (vegetable or chicken broth may be substituted)

1 teaspoon sweet **paprika**

2 tablespoons chopped fresh flat-leaf **parsley** (a handful)

In a large pot, boil potatoes in salted water until tender, about 12 minutes.

While potatoes boil, heat a large skillet over medium-high heat. Add oil to hot pan, then beef or lamb. Season with salt and pepper. Brown and crumble meat for 3 or 4 minutes. If you are using lamb and there's a lot of fat, spoon away some of the drippings. Add carrot and onion; cook 5 minutes, stirring frequently. In a second small skillet over medium heat, cook butter and flour together, 2 minutes. Whisk in broth and Worcestershire. Cook to thicken gravy 1 minute. Add gravy to meat mixture. Stir in peas.

Drain potatoes and pour them into a bowl. Combine sour cream, egg yolk, and cream. Pour the cream mixture into potatoes and mash with a masher until potatoes are almost smooth.

Preheat broiler to high. Fill a small rectangular casserole with meat and vegetable mixture. Spoon potatoes evenly over the meat. Top potatoes with paprika and broil 6 to 8 inches from the heat until evenly browned, about 2 to 3 minutes. Sprinkle with some chopped parsley and serve.

YIELD: 4 SERVINGS

5-Minute Bread Pudding

The brandy makes this a grown-ups-only recipe.

1 whole loaf **cinnamon-raisin bread**

1/4 cup (1/2 stick) **butter,** softened

1 can (14 ounces) sweetened condensed or reduced-fat **sweetened condensed milk**

2 jiggers **brandy**

Whipped cream in canister (available on dairy aisle)

Ground or grated **nutmeg,** for garnish

Heat a griddle pan over medium heat. Cut 4 thick slices cinnamon-raisin bread. Butter both sides of the bread slices with softened butter. Grill bread until brown and crispy, 2 minutes on each side.

While bread grills, make the sauce: In a small saucepan, heat condensed milk over medium-low heat for 4 minutes. Remove from heat and stir in brandy.

Cut each grilled bread slice into quarters and pile into 4 dessert cups. Top with a few spoonfuls of sauce and a generous swirl of whipped cream. Garnish cream with a sprinkle of nutmeg and serve.

YIELD: 4 SERVINGS

MENU **DECKED-OUT CLASSICS**

~ **LONG LIVE THE CHICKEN À LA KING!**

~ **ICEBERGS IN RUSSIA SALAD**

Long Live the Chicken à la King!

1 tube jumbo **bake-off biscuits,** such as Pillsbury Grands (available on dairy aisle)

A sprinkle of **cayenne** pepper (spicy) or sweet paprika (mild)

1 cup dry white **wine**

2 cups **chicken broth**

1 **bay leaf**

4 individual boneless, skinless **chicken breasts**

1 tablespoon vegetable oil or **extra-virgin olive oil** (evoo) (once around the pan)

2 tablespoons **butter**

1/2 pound small white **mushrooms,** sliced

1/2 small white **onion,** chopped

Salt and freshly ground black **pepper,** to taste

2 tablespoons all-purpose **flour**

3 tablespoons chopped **pimientos**

1 cup frozen green **peas,** thawed

2 tablespoons chopped fresh flat-leaf or curly **parsley** (a handful)

Preheat oven according to package directions for biscuits. Arrange biscuits on a nonstick baking sheet, sprinkle with a little ground cayenne pepper or sweet paprika, then bake until golden, according to package directions; remove from oven and let cool.

In a medium skillet over high heat, bring wine, chicken broth, and bay leaf to a boil. Slide in chicken breasts. When liquid returns to a boil, lower to a simmer; gently poach chicken until cooked through, 10 to 12 minutes.

Preheat a second skillet over medium heat. Add oil and butter. When butter has melted into oil, add mushrooms, onions, salt, and pepper, and cook until tender, 5 minutes. Whisk in flour and cook another minute, stirring.

Remove chicken from broth and set on cutting board. Ladle 2 to 2 & 1/2 cups cooking liquid into the mushrooms, whisking it in; discard bay leaf. Add pimientos and peas to the sauce. Dice chicken into bite-size pieces and slide into bubbling sauce. Adjust salt and pepper to taste.

Split large, warm biscuits and place bottoms on dinner plates and cover with ladles of chicken à la king, then cap with biscuit tops and garnish with chopped parsley.

YIELD: 4 SERVINGS

Icebergs in Russia Salad

4 large **eggs**
1 large head iceberg **lettuce**
1 cup **mayonnaise**
1/2 cup **ketchup** or chili sauce
1/4 cup finely chopped garlic **pickles** or half-sour pickles
Salt and freshly ground black **pepper**, to taste

Place salad plates in the freezer to quick-chill them.

Place eggs in a small, deep pot with cold water. Cover pot and when water comes to a boil, remove from heat and let eggs stand, covered, 10 minutes. Afterwards, run cold water into the pot, cooling the eggs.

Hold the lettuce head over a clean counter, core side down. Give the lettuce head a good whack on the counter and pull the core out. Quarter the head lengthwise.

Make the dressing: Combine mayonnaise, ketchup or chili sauce, and pickles. If the dressing is too thick for your liking, add a splash of water. Season with salt and pepper.

Peel and chop the hard-boiled eggs. Remove salad plates from the freezer. Place one wedge lettuce on each plate. Spill dressing over the center of the lettuce and garnish with chopped egg.

YIELD: 4 SERVINGS

MENU **WHAT A FACE!**

~ OPEN-FACED HOT TURKEY SAMMIES WITH SAUSAGE STUFFING AND GRAVY

~ SMASHED POTATOES WITH BACON

~ WARM APPLE-CRANBERRY SAUCE

Open-Faced Hot Turkey Sammies with Sausage Stuffing and Gravy, Smashed Potatoes with Bacon, Warm Apple-Cranberry Sauce

SMASHED POTATOES

2 pounds new **potatoes** or baby Yukon gold potatoes

Salt and freshly ground black **pepper,** to taste

1/2 cup **sour cream**

2 tablespoons **butter**

3 strips Ready Crisp **bacon,** crisped in microwave according to package directions and chopped

Milk or chicken broth, for thinning potatoes (optional)

WARM APPLE-CRANBERRY SAUCE

1 cup store-bought **applesauce**

1 can (14 ounces) whole berry **cranberry sauce**

STUFFING

2 slices whole-grain **bread**

1 tablespoon **butter,** softened

1 tablespoon **extra-virgin olive oil** (evoo) (once around the pan)

1 pound maple **sausage,** bulk or large links removed from casing

1 medium **onion,** chopped

2 ribs **celery,** chopped

2 teaspoons **poultry seasoning**

Salt and freshly ground black **pepper,** to taste

1 cup **chicken broth** or turkey broth

GRAVY AND TURKEY

2 tablespoons **butter**

2 tablespoons all-purpose **flour**

2 cups chicken or **turkey broth**

Salt and freshly ground black **pepper,** to taste

1 & 1/2 to 2 pounds **turkey breast** meat (rotisserie turkey breast or thick-cut deli turkey), at room temperature

4 slices whole-grain bread

2 tablespoons chopped fresh flat-leaf parsley or chives, for garnish

Preheat a medium skillet over medium-high heat.

Start the potatoes: Cut larger potatoes in half; leave smaller ones whole. Place potatoes in a medium pot. Cover with water and place over high heat with lid on. When water boils, add salt; cook potatoes with lid off until tender, 10 or 11 minutes.

Make apple-cranberry sauce: Place a second medium pot over low heat. Add applesauce and canned cranberry sauce. Stir to combine the two and gently heat through, 10 minutes.

Make the stuffing: Toast bread and butter heavily, 1/2 tablespoon per slice. Chop into small cubes and reserve.

Put a medium skillet over medium-high heat and when hot, add evoo and sausage. Brown and crumble sausage with a wooden spoon or heat-safe spatula. Add onions and celery then season with poultry seasoning, salt, and pepper; cook 5 minutes. Add bread and stir to combine. Dampen the stuffing with chicken broth and turn to combine. Turn off heat and cover pan loosely with aluminum foil.

Back to the potatoes: Drain cooked potatoes and return to hot pot. Smash with sour cream, butter, and bacon. Season with salt and pepper. If they're too thick, thin them out with a splash of milk or broth.

Make the gravy: Preheat a medium skillet over medium heat. Add 2 tablespoons butter and let it melt. Whisk in flour and cook 1 minute. Whisk in 2 cups broth. Add a pinch of salt and a few grinds of pepper. Allow gravy to thicken slightly.

Cut rotisserie meat away from the bones of turkey breast. If you are using deli turkey, remove from packaging and separate slices. Set turkey in gravy and turn to coat.

Assemble the sammies: Place a bread slice on each dinner plate. Top with a slice of turkey. Use a large ice cream scoop to place a mound of stuffing on the turkey. Place another turkey slice on top of stuffing. Serve the smashed potatoes and cranberry sauce on the side. Spoon hot extra gravy over potatoes and turkey sandwiches. Sprinkle the plates with chopped parsley or chives and serve.

YIELD: 4 SERVINGS

HE-MAN HELPINGS

Polish Stir-Fry and Pierogi Pot Stickers with Herbs and Sour Cream

My version of my friend Jon's Polish stir-fry. I highly recommend an icy cold beer in a frosted glass or beer mug with this meal.

3 tablespoons **butter,** softened

1 package (about 16 ounces) frozen **pierogi,** any brand or variety

1 cup **water**

1 & 1/2 pounds **kielbasa,** cut on an angle into large slices

1 tablespoon vegetable **oil** (once around the pan)

1 large red **onion,** quartered and sliced

1 & 1/2 pounds **kale,** trimmed and coarsely chopped

1 pound **sauerkraut,** drained

1 teaspoon ground **mustard** or 2 tablespoons prepared spicy brown mustard

1 teaspoon sweet **paprika**

Salt and freshly ground black **pepper,** to taste

2 tablespoons chopped fresh **dill** or 2 teaspoons dried dill leaves

2 tablespoons chopped fresh **chives**

2 tablespoons fresh flat-leaf **parsley,** chopped (a handful)

1 cup **sour cream**

Cover the bottom of a skillet with softened butter. Arrange pierogi in the pan in a single layer. Add 1 cup water. Cover pan and place over medium-high heat. Cook, covered, 8 minutes.

Meanwhile, heat a large nonstick skillet over medium-high heat. Brown kielbasa and remove from pan. Cover kielbasa with aluminum foil to keep warm. Drain fat and add vegetable oil; raise heat to high. Add onion and sauté for a few minutes to soften. Add kale in batches as it wilts into the pan. When done, add sauerkraut and combine. Season with mustard, paprika, salt, and pepper. Return kielbasa to pan. Toss to combine and transfer to a serving platter.

Remove lid and cook out any liquid in the pierogi pan. Let the pierogi "stick" and brown in the butter as the liquid evaporates. Remove crisp pierogi from heat and turn in chopped herbs and season with salt and pepper. Add to platter with kielbasa, and serve with sour cream on the side.

YIELD: 4 SERVINGS

MENU **RETRO-METRO TWIST ON CLASSICS**

~ MAC AND CHEDDAR CHEESE WITH CHICKEN AND BROCCOLI

~ CHOPPED ICEBERG LETTUCE WITH "FRENCH" DRESSING

Mac and Cheddar Cheese with Chicken and Broccoli

2 tablespoons **extra-virgin olive oil** (evoo)

1 pound **chicken breast tenders**, chopped

Salt and freshly ground black **pepper**, to taste

1 small **onion**, chopped

1 pound **macaroni** elbows or cavatappi (hollow, corkscrew-shaped pasta)

2 & 1/2 cups raw **broccoli** florets

3 tablespoons **butter**

3 tablespoons all-purpose **flour**

1/2 teaspoon **cayenne** pepper

1 teaspoon **paprika**

3 cups whole **milk**

1 cup **chicken broth**

2 & 1/2 cups (one 10-ounce sack) shredded sharp yellow **cheddar cheese** (preshredded is available on the dairy aisle)

1 tablespoon **Dijon** mustard

Place a large pot of water on to boil for pasta.

Meanwhile, heat a medium skillet over medium-high heat. Add evoo and chicken and season with salt and pepper. Sauté a couple of minutes then add onion; cook until onions are tender and chicken is cooked through, 5 to 7 minutes. Turn off heat and reserve.

To boiling water, add salt, then pasta. Cook 5 minutes, then add broccoli and cook for about 3 minutes.

While pasta cooks, make a roux: Heat a medium saucepan over medium heat. Add butter and let melt, then add flour, cayenne, and paprika and whisk together over heat until roux bubbles, then cook a minute more. Whisk in milk and broth and raise heat a little to bring sauce to a quick boil. Simmer to thicken, 5 minutes.

Drain pasta and broccoli florets. Add back to pot and add chicken and onions to the pasta and broccoli.

Add cheese to milk sauce and stir to melt it in, a minute or so. Stir in

mustard and season with salt and pepper. Pour sauce over chicken and broccoli and cooked pasta and stir to combine. Adjust seasonings, transfer to a large serving platter, and serve.

YIELD: 6 SERVINGS

Chopped Iceberg Lettuce with "French" Dressing

1 head iceberg **lettuce**

4 **radishes,** chopped

4 **scallions,** chopped

1/3 seedless **cucumber,** chopped

1 cup shredded **carrots** (preshredded are available in produce section)

DRESSING

1/3 cup white wine **vinegar**

1/3 cup **sugar**

1/2 cup **ketchup**

1/2 cup **extra-virgin olive oil** (evoo) (eyeball it)

1 teaspoon **garlic powder**

2 teaspoons **Worcestershire** sauce

1/4 small white **onion,** finely chopped or grated

Salt and **white pepper,** to taste

Hold the lettuce head over a clean counter, core side down. Give the lettuce head a good whack on the counter and pull the core out. Chop lettuce. Combine lettuce, radishes, scallions, cucumber, and carrots in a large salad bowl.

Make the dressing: Put all of the dressing ingredients in a blender. Put the top in place and blend on high until dressing is combined. Pour dressing over salad and toss. Adjust salt and pepper.

YIELD: 6 SERVINGS

MENU 30-MINUTE THANKFUL FEAST

~ BROWN RICE WITH HAZELNUTS

~ TURKEY CUTLETS WITH MUSHROOM–WATER CHESTNUT STUFFING AND PAN GRAVY

~ SUGAR SNAP PEAS AND CHIVES

~ SUGGESTED DESSERT: STORE-BOUGHT CHERRY OR APPLE PIE, SERVED WARM WITH VANILLA ICE CREAM

This menu can turn any day into Thanksgiving Day.

Brown Rice with Hazelnuts

1 cup chopped **hazelnuts,** such as Diamond brand (available on baking aisle)

3 cups **chicken broth**

2 tablespoons **butter** or extra-virgin olive oil (evoo)

1 & 1/2 cups **brown rice**

2 tablespoons chopped fresh flat-leaf **parsley** (a handful)

Toast nuts in a small skillet over low heat for a few minutes, then remove from heat and reserve.

Put broth and butter or evoo in a medium saucepan over high heat and bring to a boil. Add rice, stir, and return to a boil; cover and reduce heat. Simmer until tender and liquid is absorbed, 17 to 18 minutes. Remove from heat. Add nuts and parsley as you fluff rice with a fork. Transfer to serving dish.

YIELD: 6 SERVINGS

Turkey Cutlets with Mushroom-Water Chestnut Stuffing and Pan Gravy

6 slices marble rye **bread**

4 tablespoons **butter**, softened

2 & 1/2 pounds **turkey breast** cutlets

Salt and freshly ground black **pepper**, to taste

3 teaspoons **poultry seasoning**

4 tablespoons **extra-virgin olive oil** (evoo)

1 quart **turkey broth**, such as College Inn brand, or chicken broth, such as Kitchen Basics brand

2 tablespoons all-purpose **flour**

1 pound white **mushrooms**, chopped

2 ribs **celery**, from the heart, with greens, chopped

1 can (8 ounces) **water chestnuts** (1 cup), drained and chopped

1/2 **red bell pepper**, seeded and chopped

3 **scallions**, chopped

2 tablespoons fresh **thyme** leaves, chopped

2 tablespoons chopped fresh flat-leaf **parsley** (a handful)

Preheat broiler to high and toast bread on both sides. Use 2 tablespoons of the butter to spread liberally on the toast. Switch oven to bake and preheat to 375°F.

Season turkey cutlets with salt, pepper, and 2 teaspoons of the poultry seasoning (eyeball it). In a large skillet over medium-high heat, heat 2 tablespoons evoo; brown turkey cutlets in evoo, about 2 minutes on each side. Transfer cutlets to a shallow baking dish and add 1 cup broth to keep meat moist. Tent cutlets loosely with aluminum foil and transfer to oven.

Make the gravy: To the same skillet, add the remaining 2 tablespoons butter and let it melt over medium heat. Add flour and cook a minute or two more. Whisk in 2 cups broth and allow gravy to thicken, 5 minutes. Season with salt and pepper and remaining teaspoon of poultry seasoning.

Preheat a second skillet over medium-high heat and add the remaining 2 tablespoons evoo. Add mushrooms and brown 5 minutes, stirring frequently. Season mushrooms with salt and pepper. Add celery, water chestnuts, and bell pepper. Continue to cook until veggies are all tender, another 5 minutes. Add scallions, thyme, and parsley. Cut toast into cubes and add to skillet. Moisten stuffing with 1 cup broth. Transfer to a serving dish. Use an ice cream scoop to portion out the stuffing at the table. Top mounds of stuffing with turkey cutlets and gravy.

YIELD: 6 SERVINGS

Sugar Snap Peas and Chives

1 & 1/2 pounds sugar **snap peas**

Salt, to taste

1 teaspoon **sugar**

2 tablespoons **butter**

3 tablespoons chopped or snipped fresh **chives**

Place peas in a pot and add 1 inch water. Add a little salt, the sugar, and butter to the pot. Bring water to a boil. Reduce heat to simmer. Cover and cook until peas are tender but still bright green, 7 to 8 minutes. Remove from heat and add chives. Transfer peas to a serving dish.

YIELD: 6 SERVINGS

MENU NOT-YOUR-AVERAGE STEAK

~ PEPPER STEAK AND RICE PILAF WITH MUSHROOMS
~ MIXED SALAD WITH "HOUSE DRESSING"

Pepper Steak and Rice Pilaf with Mushrooms

RICE PILAF WITH MUSHROOMS

1 tablespoon **extra-virgin olive oil** (evoo) (once around the pan)
1 tablespoon **butter**
10 white **mushrooms**, chopped
1 & 3/4 cups **water**
1 package (6 ounces) **rice pilaf mix**, such as Near East brand
2 tablespoons chopped fresh flat-leaf **parsley** (a handful)

PEPPER STEAK

2 tablespoons vegetable **oil** (twice around the pan)
2 pounds **beef tenderloin tips** or sirloin, cut into chunks
Salt, to taste
2 tablespoons **butter**
2 **green bell peppers**, seeded, cut into 2-inch dice
1/2 white **onion**, sliced
2 tablespoons all-purpose **flour**
1/4 cup dry **sherry** (eyeball it)
1 & 1/2 cups **beef consommé**
1 tablespoon **tomato paste**
1 teaspoon freshly ground black **pepper**

Make the pilaf: In a medium pot over medium heat add evoo and butter. When butter has melted, add mushrooms and sauté 3 to 5 minutes. Add water, cover the pot, and bring to a quick boil. Add rice and spice packet. Stir to combine, reduce heat, and cook 18 minutes. Add parsley, fluff with fork.

Make the pepper steak: Preheat a large skillet over high heat. Add vegetable oil to really hot pan. Add meat and sear on all sides, 5 minutes. Season with salt and remove to a plate. Cover meat loosely with aluminum foil. Reduce heat to medium. Add butter to pan. Add bell peppers and onions; sauté 5 minutes. Sprinkle flour over vegetables and cook 1 minute longer. Whisk in sherry, scraping up pan drippings. Whisk in consommé. Whisk in tomato paste and black pepper. Slide meat back into the pan and coat with sauce. Reduce heat to low and simmer 5 minutes.

Spoon pepper steak over rice pilaf and serve.

YIELD: 4 SERVINGS

Mixed Salad with "House Dressing"

1 sack (10 ounces) chopped **romaine** and mixed greens
4 **radishes,** sliced
3 tablespoons **vinegar,** any kind
1 teaspoon **sugar**
1 teaspoon sweet **paprika**
1 tablespoon grated white **onion** and its juice
1/3 cup **extra-virgin olive oil** (evoo)
Salt and freshly ground black **pepper,** to taste
2 tablespoons **sesame seeds** (optional)

Mix greens and radishes in a large salad bowl. In a small bowl, combine vinegar, sugar, paprika, and onion with juice. Whisk in evoo. Season the dressing with salt and pepper. Dress and toss salad then sprinkle with sesame seeds (if desired) and serve.

YIELD: 4 SERVINGS

MENU GO FISH!

~ BAKED STUFFED FLOUNDER

~ LONG-GRAIN AND WILD RICE WITH ARTICHOKES

Baked Stuffed Flounder

1 tablespoon **extra-virgin olive oil** (evoo) (once around the pan)

2 slices **bacon**, chopped

1 medium **onion**, finely chopped

1 **shallot**, finely chopped

2 cloves **garlic**, chopped

1/4 **red bell pepper**, finely chopped

1 rib **celery** with greens, finely chopped

Salt and freshly ground black **pepper**, to taste

1/2 teaspoon ground **thyme**

3 tablespoons chopped fresh flat-leaf **parsley**

6 ounces **crabmeat**, flaked

1/4 cup **butter** (1/2 stick), cut into pieces

4 large **flounder fillets** (1 & 1/3 pounds total)

1 **lemon**, cut into wedges

1/2 cup **bread crumbs**

A sprinkle of sweet **paprika**, for garnish

Preheat oven to 400°F.

Heat a medium skillet over medium-high heat; add evoo and bacon and cook until bacon begins to crisp, 2 to 3 minutes. Add onion, shallot, garlic, bell pepper, celery, salt, pepper, thyme, and 2 tablespoons parsley. Sauté 2 minutes. Stir in crabmeat and remove from heat.

Heat a second medium skillet over medium heat. Add butter and let it melt. Season flounder with salt and squeeze a little lemon juice on both sides. Turn fish in melted butter and set on a shallow baking pan or sheet pan. Add bread crumbs to the melted butter and cook, stirring, until brown. Add the crab and vegetable mixture to the bread crumbs and combine. Mound stuffing on half of each flounder fillet and fold fillets over to wrap and seal the stuffing. Bake until fish is opaque, about 20 minutes. Serve with remaining lemon wedges, garnished with the remaining tablespoon parsley and a sprinkle of paprika.

YIELD: 4 SERVINGS

Long-Grain and Wild Rice with Artichokes

1 & 3/4 cups **chicken broth**

1 tablespoon **extra-virgin olive oil** (evoo)

1 tablespoon **butter**, cut in half

1 package (6 ounces) long-grain and **wild rice**, such as Near East brand

1 clove **garlic**, crushed

1 can (15 ounces) small **artichoke hearts**, drained and halved

Salt and freshly ground black **pepper**, to taste

2 tablespoons chopped fresh flat-leaf **parsley** (a handful)

Place chicken broth, half a tablespoon evoo (eyeball it), and half a tablespoon butter in a small pot; bring to a boil. Add spice packet and rice and return to a boil. Cover, reduce heat to simmer, and cook 17 minutes.

To a small skillet over medium heat add remaining half tablespoon each evoo and butter. Add garlic and cook a minute, then add artichokes, season with a little salt and pepper, and cook 5 minutes.

Portion out cooked rice on dinner plates and top with artichokes and a generous sprinkling of parsley. Serve alongside flounder.

YIELD: 4 SERVINGS

MENU **ITALIAN STICK-TO-YOUR-RIBS**

~ **ITALIAN MINI-MEAT LOAVES WITH MAC 'N THREE CHEESES**
~ **SEARED GREENS WITH RED ONION AND VINEGAR**

Italian Mini-Meat Loaves with Mac 'n Three Cheeses

MEAT LOAVES

1 & 1/3 pounds **ground sirloin**

1 large **egg,** beaten

2/3 cup Italian **bread crumbs** (a couple of handfuls)

1/4 cup grated **Parmigiano** Reggiano cheese (a handful)

1/2 small **green bell pepper,** chopped

1/2 small **onion,** finely chopped

4 cloves **garlic,** chopped

3 tablespoons **tomato paste**

Salt and freshly ground black **pepper**

2 tablespoons **extra-virgin olive oil** (evoo)

MAC 'N CHEESE

1 pound **cavatappi** (hollow, corkscrew-shaped pasta) or small shell pasta

2 tablespoons **butter**

2 tablespoon all-purpose **flour**

2 cups **milk**

2 cups shredded sharp **cheddar** cheese

1/2 cup shredded **Asiago** cheese

1/2 cup grated **Parmigiano** Reggiano cheese

1 teaspoon coarse black **pepper**

1/2 cup Italian **bread crumbs**

2 tablespoons **extra-virgin olive oil** (evoo)

2 tablespoons chopped fresh **thyme**

2–3 tablespoons chopped fresh **rosemary**

1/4 cup chopped fresh flat-leaf **parsley**

Put a large pot of water on to boil. Preheat oven to 425°F.

Place meat in a bowl. Make a well in meat. Fill well with egg, bread crumbs, 1/4 cup Parmigiano Reggiano cheese, bell pepper, onion, garlic, tomato paste, salt, and pepper. Mix meat and breading and form 4 individual oval meat loaves, about 1-inch thick. Coat loaves with 2 tablespoons evoo and arrange on a baking sheet. Roast 18 to 20 minutes.

When done, remove meat and switch oven heat to broiler.

When the pasta water boils, add salt then pasta. Cook until slightly undercooked—pasta will continue to cook when combined with cheese sauce.

Melt butter in a saucepan and stir in flour. Whisk in milk. Bring to a bubble. Cook to thicken milk, 2 to 3 minutes. Add cheddar, Asiago, Parmigiano Reggiano, and black pepper. Stir to melt cheeses. Drain pasta and combine with cheese sauce and transfer to a baking dish or casserole. Place bread crumbs in a bowl, add evoo, thyme, rosemary, and parsley. Stir to combine and top the pasta and cheese. Place under broiler to brown bread crumbs. Serve mac and cheese alongside meat loaves.

YIELD: 4 SERVINGS

Seared Greens with Red Onion and Vinegar

2 tablespoons vegetable or other light **oil** (twice around the pan)

1/2 red **onion**, sliced

1 teaspoon **mustard seed**

1 & 1/2 to 2 pounds red or yellow Swiss **chard**, stems removed and tops coarsely chopped

1/4 cup red wine **vinegar**

Salt and freshly ground black **pepper**, to taste

Heat a large skillet over high heat. Add oil then onion and mustard seeds. Sear onion and mustard seeds, 2 minutes. Add greens and toss with tongs in oil. Sear greens 2 to 3 minutes. Add vinegar and toss with greens. Remove pan from heat and season greens with salt and pepper.

YIELD: 4 SERVINGS

MENU SICILIAN STICK-TO-YOUR-RIBS

~ MEAT LOAF BRASCIOLE (ROLL-UPS)

~ PASTA WITH BROCCOLINI AND RICOTTA

Meat Loaf Brasciole (Roll-Ups)

1 & 1/2 pounds **meat loaf mix** (ground beef, pork, and veal) (available at the butcher's counter)

Salt and freshly ground black **pepper**

1/2 cup Italian **bread crumbs**

1 **egg**

2 cloves **garlic**, minced

1/2 small white **onion**, finely chopped

2 tablespoons golden **raisins**, chopped

3 tablespoons **pine nuts**, chopped

3 tablespoons grated **Parmigiano** Reggiano or Romano cheese

2 tablespoons chopped fresh flat-leaf **parsley** (a handful)

1 cup **arugula** or baby spinach

6 slices **prosciutto** di Parma

6 deli slices **provolone** cheese

Preheat oven to 450°F.

Mix meat, salt, pepper, bread crumbs, egg, garlic, onions, raisins, pine nuts, Parmigiano, and parsley as if you were making meat loaf. Flatten meat out on a cookie sheet into a thin layer, 1/2-inch thick, 12-inches long by 6- to 8-inches wide. Cover meat with arugula or spinach, prosciutto, and provolone. Roll the meat up into a large log, working across the shorter side so that you have a 12-inch-long log.

Roast 20 minutes. Cut into 1-inch slices, 3 pieces per portion, and serve.

YIELD: 4 SERVINGS

Pasta with Broccolini and Ricotta

Salt and freshly ground black **pepper,** to taste

1/2 pound **cavatappi** (hollow, corkscrew-shaped pasta) or rigatoni

1 pound **broccolini,** trimmed into florets

1 cup **water**

A drizzle of **extra-virgin olive oil** (evoo)

2 tablespoons **butter**

1 cup **ricotta** cheese

2 teaspoons grated **lemon zest**

1/2 cup grape or small vine **tomatoes,** halved

2 tablespoons fresh **thyme** leaves

Bring water in a large pot to a boil; add salt and pasta and cook until pasta is al dente (with a bite to it), 7 to 8 minutes. Drain pasta and return it to hot pot.

While pasta is cooking, place broccolini in a small pan and add 1 cup water and some salt. Bring to a boil; cover and cook 5 minutes. Drain and reserve.

To hot cooked pasta add evoo, butter, ricotta, and lemon zest. Toss pasta to coat it in the cheese and butter. Season with salt. Portion pasta onto dinner plates alongside brasciole and top with cooked broccolini, cut tomatoes, lots of fresh thyme, and a few grinds of pepper.

YIELD: 4 SERVINGS

MENU A FAVORITE-OF-MY-FAMILY

~ SCUDERI KIDS' FAST, FAKE-BAKED ZITI

~ SPINACH AND ARTICHOKE SALAD

Scuderi Kids' Fast, Fake-Baked Ziti

My mom (and her nine brothers and sisters, I'm sure) loved ziti al forno: ziti and red sauce with béchamel (white sauce) and cheese on top, slow-baked in the oven. This is a ziti I'm sure the kids would have loved even more 'cause this fake-out only takes 30 minutes to cook! If San Marzano tomatoes are not available, you might want to add a teaspoon of sugar to your sauce.

3 tablespoons **extra-virgin olive oil** (evoo) (3 times around pan)

3 cloves **garlic**, finely chopped

1 can (28 ounces) **whole peeled tomatoes**, preferably San Marzano

1 can (14 ounces) **crushed tomatoes**, preferably San Marzano

Salt and freshly ground black **pepper**, to taste

A handful of fresh **basil** leaves, torn

1 pound **ziti rigate**

2 tablespoons **butter**

2 tablespoons all-purpose **flour**

A generous grating of fresh **nutmeg**

2 cups whole **milk**

1/2 cup shredded **Asiago** cheese

1/2 cup shredded **Parmigiano** Reggiano cheese

1 cup cubed fresh **mozzarella** cheese

Crusty **bread**, to pass at table

Put a large pot of water on to boil. Preheat the broiler.

Heat a medium saucepan over medium heat; add evoo, then garlic. Sauté garlic a minute or two; do not let the garlic brown. Chop whole tomatoes and add them to the pan. Add crushed tomatoes and salt and simmer 10 minutes. Add basil and simmer over low heat 10 minutes more.

When water boils, add salt and pasta and cook 6 minutes, leaving pasta a little chewy.

While pasta cooks, make the béchamel sauce: Melt butter in a small pot over medium heat. Whisk in flour, then salt, pepper, and nutmeg; cook 1 minute. Stir in milk and bring sauce to a bubble. Cook 5 minutes to reduce.

When pasta is cooked, drain and transfer to a big casserole dish. Pour the tomato and basil sauce over the pasta and turn to coat the pasta. Pour the béchamel over pasta—do not mix. Cover the top of the pasta with Asiago, Parmigiano, and mozzarella. Place the casserole under hot broiler and melt cheese until brown and bubbly, 3 to 5 minutes. Serve immediately.

YIELD: 6 SERVINGS

Spinach and Artichoke Salad

3/4 pound (4–5 packed cups) fresh baby **spinach** leaves

2 cans (15 ounces each) artichoke hearts packed in water, drained and sliced

1 clove **garlic**, finely chopped

2 teaspoons grated **lemon zest**

1 tablespoon **lemon juice**

2 tablespoons red wine **vinegar**

1/4 to 1/3 cup **extra-virgin olive oil** (evoo)

Salt and freshly ground black **pepper**, to taste

A handful of shredded **Parmigiano** Reggiano cheese

Combine spinach and artichokes. Place garlic in a small dish and add lemon zest, lemon juice, and vinegar. Let stand 5 minutes then whisk in evoo. Pour dressing over salad and toss to combine. Season with salt and pepper. Top with cheese then serve.

YIELD: 6 SERVINGS

MENU BEST OF THE BOOT

~ BUCATINI ALL'AMATRICIANA

~ VEAL CHOPS WITH PEPPERS AND ONIONS

~ SUGGESTED DESSERT: NEAPOLITAN ICE CREAM AND ITALIAN COOKIES FOR KIDS, VIN SANTO AFTER-DINNER WINE AND BISCOTTI FOR ADULTS

Bucatini all'Amatriciana

2 tablespoons **extra-virgin olive oil** (evoo) (twice around the pan)

1/4 pound (4 or 5 slices) **pancetta**, chopped

1 medium **onion**, chopped

4–6 cloves **garlic**, chopped

1 teaspoon crushed **red pepper flakes**

1 can (28 ounces) **crushed tomatoes**

2 tablespoons chopped fresh flat-leaf **parsley** (a handful)

Salt and freshly ground black **pepper**, to taste

1 pound **bucatini** (hollow spaghetti)

Grated **Parmigiano** Reggiano, grana padano, or Romano **cheese**, to pass at table

Bring a large pot of water to a boil.

Meanwhile, heat a large, deep skillet over medium-high heat. Add evoo and pancetta. Cook pancetta 2 or 3 minutes then add onions, garlic, and crushed red pepper flakes. Cook until onions are translucent, 7 or 8 minutes. Add tomatoes and parsley. Season with salt and pepper. Simmer sauce over low heat until ready to serve.

Add salt and pasta to boiling water. Cook pasta to al dente (with a bite to it), about 10 minutes. Drain pasta well. Do not rinse; starchy pasta holds more sauce. Toss hot pasta with sauce and serve. Pass grated cheese at the table.

* Pancetta is Italian rolled, cured pork, similar to bacon, but not smoked. Look for it at your deli counter. Bacon may be substituted; it will result in a smoky-tasting tomato sauce.

YIELD: 6 SERVINGS

Veal Chops with Peppers and Onions

4 bone-in **veal chops** (1/2-inch thick)

Salt and freshly ground black **pepper,** to taste

3 tablespoons **extra-virgin olive oil** (evoo) (3 times around the pan)

4 cloves **garlic,** smashed away from skins

3 **cubanelles** (Italian sweet peppers), sliced

1/2 cup dry white **wine**

2 **hot cherry peppers,** chopped

2–3 tablespoons **juice from cherry pepper** jar (a splash)

Chopped fresh flat-leaf **parsley,** for garnish

Preheat oven to 375°F.

Heat a skillet with an ovenproof handle over medium-high heat. (If you don't have an ovenproof skillet, double-wrap the handle tightly in aluminum foil.) Season chops with salt and pepper. To hot skillet, add 2 tablespoons evoo, then the chops. Brown chops 2 minutes on each side; remove to a plate.

Add the remaining tablespoon evoo to the pan, then the garlic and sweet peppers. Cook until soft, 3 to 5 minutes, then add the wine. Return chops to the pan with the peppers and transfer the pan to the oven. Cook chops and peppers 12 to 15 minutes or until juices run clear near the bone. Remove pan from oven and add cherry peppers and a splash of pepper juice. Transfer chops to a serving platter. Spoon juices and peppers evenly over the chops and garnish with parsley.

YIELD: 4 SERVINGS

MENU NOT-JUST-ANOTHER CHICKEN AND RICE DINNER

~ CHEESY RISI E BISI (ARBORIO RICE AND PEAS)

~ CRISPY CHICKEN CUTLETS WITH BASIL-PARSLEY SAUCE

Cheesy Risi e Bisi

2 tablespoons **extra-virgin olive oil** (evoo) (twice around the pan)

1 large clove **garlic,** finely chopped

1 small **onion,** finely chopped

1 cup **Arborio rice**

Salt and freshly ground black **pepper,** to taste

1/2 cup dry white **wine**

3–4 cups **chicken broth**

1/4 to 1/3 cup grated **Parmigiano** Reggiano cheese (a generous handful)

2 tablespoons chopped fresh flat-leaf **parsley** (a handful)

1 cup tiny frozen **peas,** thawed

Heat a medium skillet over medium-high heat. Add evoo then garlic and onion and sauté, stirring constantly, 2 to 3 minutes. Add rice and season with a little salt and pepper. Cook another minute or so, then add wine and cook until wine is completely absorbed, 30 seconds. Add about 1 cup chicken broth and stir. Reduce heat to medium and cook until broth is absorbed, stirring often. Continue adding 1/2 cup broth each time liquid becomes completely absorbed, stirring all the while. Use as much broth as is necessary to result in creamy, slightly chewy rice; this should take about 22 minutes. Work on chicken while rice continues to cook; recipe follows.

When rice is cooked to desired consistency, remove from heat and stir in cheese, parsley, and peas and stir to combine and to heat peas through.

YIELD: 4 SERVINGS

Crispy Chicken Cutlets with Basil-Parsley Sauce

2 pounds **chicken cutlets**

Salt and freshly ground black **pepper**

3–4 tablespoons all-purpose **flour**

1 cup Italian **bread crumbs**

1/3 to 1/2 cup grated **Parmigiano** Reggiano cheese (a couple of handfuls)

1 teaspoon crushed **red pepper flakes**

2 teaspoons **poultry seasoning** (half a palmful)

1 clove **garlic**

1 jar (3 ounces) **pine nuts** (pignoli)

Grated zest of 1 **lemon** (2 tablespoons)

2 **eggs**, beaten

Olive oil, for frying

1 plum **tomato**, seeded and finely chopped, for garnish

SAUCE

1 cup loosely packed **basil** leaves

1/2 cup loosely packed fresh flat-leaf **parsley** leaves

Juice of 1/2 **lemon**

Salt and freshly ground black **pepper**, to taste

1/4 cup **extra-virgin olive oil** (evoo) (eyeball it)

Season cutlets with salt and pepper on both sides. Place flour in a shallow dish and turn cutlets lightly in flour.

Combine bread crumbs, cheese, red pepper flakes, poultry seasoning, garlic, pine nuts, and lemon zest in a food processor and pulse-process to evenly mix. Transfer the mixture to a plate. Beat eggs in a separate shallow dish.

Heat a thin layer of oil, just enough to coat the bottom of the pan, in a large skillet over medium to medium-high heat. Coat cutlets in eggs then breading and place in hot oil. Cook cutlets in a single layer, in 2 batches if necessary, until breading is evenly browned and cutlets' juices run clear, 3 or 4 minutes on each side. Remove to a plate and tent with aluminum foil to keep warm.

Make the sauce: Return food processor bowl to base and add basil, parsley, and lemon juice. Add a little salt and pepper. Turn processor on and stream in evoo until a loose paste forms.

Serve chicken cutlets with a generous topping of basil and parsley sauce. Garnish with tomato.

YIELD: 4 SERVINGS

MENU **SOUP AND SAMMY NIGHT**

~ CREAMY TOMATO-BASIL SOUP

~ ITALIAN PATTY MELTS

Creamy Tomato-Basil Soup and Italian Patty Melts

SOUP

4 cups whole **milk**

3 cans (14 ounces each) **diced tomatoes**, drained

2 rounded tablespoons **tomato paste**

1 medium **onion**, chopped

Salt and freshly ground black **pepper**, to taste

1 teaspoon **sugar**

1/4 cup all-purpose **flour**

2 tablespoons **butter**, cut into pieces

1 rib **celery**, coarsely chopped

1 clove **garlic**

1/2 cup store-bought **basil pesto** (available on dairy aisle)

PATTY MELTS

1 tablespoon **extra-virgin olive oil** (evoo), plus more for drizzling

4 sweet Italian **sausage** patties (1/4 pound each) (available in packaged meat case)

1 **cubanelle** (sweet Italian pepper), seeded and sliced

1 medium **onion**, sliced

Salt and freshly ground black **pepper**, to taste

8 slices sliced Italian **bread**

8 deli slices **provolone** cheese

Make the soup: Pour milk into a medium pot over medium heat and heat until hot but not boiling. Put tomatoes, tomato paste, onions, salt, pepper, sugar, flour, butter, celery, and garlic in a food processor and grind until smooth. Pour mixture into hot milk and raise heat to bring soup to a boil. Reduce heat and simmer 15 minutes.

Start the patty melts: Heat a nonstick skillet over medium-high heat. Drizzle the pan with evoo and add sausage patties; cook 5 minutes on each side. Remove from the pan and add another tablespoon evoo and the peppers and onions. Season with salt and pepper and cook until peppers and onions are just tender, about 5 minutes. Remove them from the pan. Wipe pan clean and reduce heat to medium-low.

Assemble the sandwiches: Place 4 slices bread on a work surface, top each with 1/4 of the peppers and onions, then a slice of cheese, a sausage patty, another slice of cheese, and another slice of bread. Add butter to skillet and cook patty melts until golden and cheese is melted, 2 or 3 minutes on each side. Press with spatula as they cook or set another heavy skillet on top to weigh them down.

Pour soup into shallow bowls and stir a couple of rounded spoonfuls of pesto into each serving. Cut the patty melts corner to corner and dip in the soup as you eat.

YIELD: 4 SERVINGS

Thicker than soups, not as heavy as stews, "stoups" are perfectly comforting and do-able for any night of the busy week!

"STOUPS"

~ ZUPPA OSSO BUCO

~ CHICKEN PROVENÇAL "STOUP"

~ HUNGARIAN HOT SAUSAGE AND LENTIL "STOUP"

Zuppa Osso Buco

This stoup tastes like osso buco: slow-braised veal shanks and vegetables, topped with gremolata—a lemon, anchovy, and garlic topping that adds a bright, nutty flavor. In 30 minutes, you won't believe the slow-cooked flavor of this "stoup"; it is possibly my favorite dish in this book!

VEAL DUMPLINGS

1 pound **ground veal**

1 large **egg**, beaten

1/3 cup Italian **bread crumbs** (a couple of handfuls)

1/4 cup grated **Parmigiano** Reggiano or Romano cheese (a generous handful)

1/4 to 1/2 teaspoon freshly grated **nutmeg** (eyeball it)

Salt and freshly ground black **pepper**

STOUP

2 **carrots**, peeled

2 ribs **celery** with greens

1 medium **onion**

2 tablespoons **extra-virgin olive oil** (evoo) (twice around the pot)

Salt and freshly ground black **pepper**, to taste

1 fresh or dried **bay leaf**

1/2 cup white **wine**

1 can (14 ounces) **cannellini** (white beans), drained

1 can (15 ounces) diced **tomatoes in purée** or coarsely ground tomatoes

3 cups **chicken broth**

2 cups **beef stock** or broth

1 cup egg **pasta**, such as egg fettucine (broken into pieces) or medium egg noodles

GREMOLATA

2 cloves **garlic**, cracked away from skins

6–8 **anchovies** (1 tin flat fillets, 2 ounces), drained

1/4 cup loosely packed fresh flat-leaf **parsley** leaves (a handful)

Grated zest of 1 lemon (2 tablespoons)
Crusty bread, to pass at table

Start the dumplings: Combine veal, egg, bread crumbs, cheese, nutmeg, salt, and pepper in a bowl; reserve. Wash your hands.

Make the stoup: Heat a medium soup pot over medium heat. Chop veggies while pot heats up: dice carrots into 1/4-inch pieces, chop celery and onion. Add evoo to hot pot, then add carrots. Turn carrots to coat them in oil and add celery and onions. Work near the stove so you can chop, then drop veggies into the pot. Season with salt and pepper; add bay leaf. Stir and cook to begin to soften, about 5 minutes. Do not let vegetables brown; reduce heat if necessary. Add wine, beans, tomatoes, chicken broth, and beef stock to the pot. Put a lid on the pot and raise heat to high.

Start rolling dumpling mixture into 1-inch balls. When soup boils, about 3 minutes, add dumplings directly to the pot. Stir in egg noodles. Simmer to cook noodles and meat dumplings, 6 minutes. Adjust seasonings and turn the heat off, then let stoup stand a couple of minutes.

Make gremolata: Pile garlic, anchovies, parsley, and lemon zest on a cutting board and finely chop together, then transfer to a small dish.

Serve stoup in shallow bowls with a couple of teaspoonfuls of gremolata on top. Let everyone stir the gremolata throughout their stoup; pass crusty bread at the table for dipping and mopping.

YIELD: 4 SERVINGS

Chicken Provençal "Stoup"

2 medium **carrots**

2 tablespoons **extra-virgin olive oil** (evoo) (twice around the pan)

2 cloves **garlic,** chopped

1 medium **zucchini**

1 small to medium **red bell pepper,** seeded

1 medium **onion,** peeled and halved

Salt and freshly ground black **pepper,** to taste

1 tablespoon **herbes de Provence** (available on spice aisle) or 1 teaspoon each dried sage, rosemary, and thyme

1 & 1/2 pounds small red-skinned **potatoes**

1 cup dry white **wine**

1 can (14 ounces) diced tomatoes or coarsely **ground tomatoes**

1 quart plus 1 cup **chicken broth**

1 pound **chicken tenders,** diced

1 small jar (4 ounces) **black olive tapenade** (available on condiment aisle)

2 tablespoons chopped fresh flat-leaf **parsley** (a handful)

Crusty **bread,** to pass at table

Heat a medium soup pot over medium-high heat. While soup pot heats, chop carrots into 1/4-inch dice. Pour evoo into pot, then add garlic and carrots and stir to coat in evoo. Chop zucchini, bell peppers, and onions, all diced into 1/2-inch pieces. Season all the veggies with salt, pepper, and herbes de Provence. Cook 5 minutes. While they cook, cut potatoes into thin wedges. Add wine to vegetables and reduce a minute or so. Add tomatoes, potatoes, and broth. Cover the pot and raise heat to high. Bring the stoup to a boil, then add chicken and simmer until potatoes are just tender and chicken is cooked through, 8 to 10 minutes. Serve stoup in shallow bowls and stir in a rounded spoonful of tapenade at the table. Top soup with chopped parsley and pass crusty bread for dipping and mopping.

YIELD: 4 SERVINGS

COOKING 'ROUND THE CLOCK

Hungarian Hot Sausage and Lentil "Stoup"

2 tablespoons **extra-virgin olive oil** (evoo) (twice around the pan)

1 & 1/2 pounds bulk hot Italian **sausage**

3 cloves **garlic**, chopped

1 medium **onion**, chopped

2 portobello **mushrooms**, gills scraped out, chopped

1 cup shredded **carrots** (preshredded are available in produce section)

1 cup **lentils**

1 large starchy **potato**, peeled and chopped

Salt and freshly ground black **pepper**, to taste

1 **bay leaf**, fresh or dried

2 teaspoons hot smoked **paprika** or 1 tablespoon cumin, 1 teaspoon sweet paprika, and 1/2 teaspoon cayenne pepper

3 stems fresh **rosemary**

1 can (14 ounces) finely **diced tomatoes** or chunky-style crushed tomatoes

6 cups **chicken broth**

4 cups **kale** or chard, shredded and chopped

Crusty pumpernickel **bread**, to pass at table

Butter, for bread

Heat a medium soup pot over medium-high heat. Add evoo and meat to the pot. Brown meat 2 or 3 minutes, then chop and add garlic, onions, and mushrooms. Cook a few minutes then add carrots, lentils, potatoes, salt, pepper, bay leaf, paprika, and rosemary (rosemary leaves will fall off the stems as the soup cooks). Add tomatoes and broth and cover the pot. Raise heat to high to bring to a fast boil, then remove lid. Stir in kale or chard and boil until the lentils are just tender, 15 minutes. Remove rosemary stems. Serve stoup in shallow bowls and pass pumpernickel bread and butter to dip and mop up the stoup.

YIELD: 4 SERVINGS

MENU COUNTRY INN SUPPER

~ BEEF AND WATERCRESS DUMPLING "STOUP"

~ HOT SPIKED CIDER

~ MAPLE-WALNUT ICE CREAM CUPS

Beef and Watercress Dumpling "Stoup"

2 pounds **beef sirloin** (1-inch thick), trimmed

2 tablespoons vegetable **oil** (twice around the pan)

4 slices hickory- or applewood-smoked **bacon**, chopped

2 medium **onions**, chopped

4 ribs **celery**, chopped

2 fresh or dried **bay leaves**

4 sprigs fresh **thyme** or 1 teaspoon dried

2 tablespoons all-purpose **flour**

1 cup dry red **wine** (eyeball it)

1 rounded tablespoon spicy brown **mustard** or grainy Dijon mustard

1 quart **beef broth** or stock

1/4 to 1/2 teaspoon **Liquid Smoke** (optional)

Salt and freshly ground black **pepper**, to taste

1 box **biscuit mix** (5 to 6 ounces) such as Jiffy brand

1 cup chopped **watercress**

Heat a large, wide heavy-bottomed pot or pan over high heat. Cut the sirloin into large cubes. Add oil to the pan, then add meat. Sear meat until caramelized, 2 minutes on each side. Remove to a shallow dish and tent with aluminum foil. Reduce heat to medium-high. Add bacon to the pan and cook until brown at edges, rendering fat. Add onions, celery, bay, and thyme. Stir and cook 5 minutes. Sprinkle in flour, stir, and cook another minute. Whisk in wine and mustard and scrape up pan drippings. Add broth. Cover and bring liquid to a boil, 1 to 2 minutes.

Mix biscuit mix according to package directions, adding watercress at the beginning. Add meat back to the pan and settle it in so that it is covered with sauce. Add liquid smoke (if using) and season with salt and pepper. Drop large spoonfuls of watercress dumpling mix onto the surface of the stew and cover the pan. Cook until dumplings are plump and cooked through, about 8 minutes. Serve hot.

YIELD: 4 SERVINGS

Hot Spiked Cider

2 quarts apple cider
2 cloves
2 cinnamon sticks
8 shots apple brandy

In a large pot over medium-high heat, heat cider with cloves and cinnamon. Pour 2 shots of apple brandy into each of 4 mugs and fill with cider.

YIELD: 4 SERVINGS

Maple-Walnut Ice Cream Cups

1 cup pure maple syrup
1 cup granola
2 pints maple-walnut ice cream
Whipped cream, from a canister (available on dairy aisle)
Ground cinnamon, for sprinkling
1/2 cup chopped walnuts

Place syrup in a small pitcher or cup and microwave on high to warm, 15 seconds.

Place 1/4 cup granola in each of 4 small dessert cups or bowls. Drizzle with syrup. Add 2 scoops ice cream each. Top with whipped cream, another drizzle of syrup, a sprinkle of cinnamon, and chopped nuts. Serve.

YIELD: 4 SERVINGS

MENU HOT MAMACITA

~ TURKEY, CHORIZO, AND CHIPOTLE "STOUP" WITH CORN CAKES
~ COOL-IT-DOWN CRANBERRY MARGARITAS

Turkey, Chorizo, and Chipotle "Stoup" with Corn Cakes

2 tablespoons **extra-virgin olive oil** (evoo), corn oil, or vegetable oil (twice around the pan)

1/2 pound **chorizo**, chopped

2 pounds ground **turkey breast**

1 medium **onion**, chopped

3 cloves **garlic**, chopped

1 rounded tablespoon **chili powder** (a palmful)

2 **chipotles** in adobo, chopped (available on Spanish or Mexican foods aisle) or 1/2 cup hot chipotle salsa

Salt, to taste

1 cup Mexican **beer**

2 cups **chicken broth**

1 can (28 ounces) chopped **stewed tomatoes**

1 can (15 ounces) red **kidney beans**, drained

1 package (5 ounces) Jiffy brand **corn muffin mix**

8 ounces pepper-Jack **cheese**, shredded (1 & 1/2 cups)

2 tablespoons **butter**

Heat a deep skillet or wide pot over medium-high heat. Add oil and chorizo, brown 1 minute. Push chorizo off to the side and add turkey to the pan. Brown turkey, crumbling meat as it cooks, 3 minutes. Add onions, garlic, chili powder, and chipotles. Cook another 5 minutes. Season with salt. Add beer and cook another minute, stirring to loosen any bits from the bottom of the pan. Add broth, tomatoes, and beans. Bring to a bubble. Reduce heat and simmer 10 minutes.

Heat a nonstick griddle pan over medium-high heat. Mix corn muffin mix according to package directions for corn cakes. Mix in cheese. Nest butter in a paper towel and rub grill with butter. Ladle batter onto griddle in 3-inch cakes; cook until golden, 3 minutes on each side. Transfer corn cakes to a plate and tent with aluminum foil to keep warm.

Pour stoup into bowls and top with cheese-corn cakes—like a spicy, corn-topped chili pot pie.

YIELD: 4 SERVINGS (WITH LEFTOVERS)

Cool-It-Down Cranberry Margaritas

1 container (10 ounces) frozen **limeade** or margarita mix, such as Bacardi brand

1 tray **ice cubes**

8 shots **tequila**

1 can **cranberry juice concentrate** or cranapple juice concentrate, such as Mott's brand

Combine all ingredients in a blender and blend on high. If your blender is small or not high-powered, divide ingredients into two batches. Pour into margarita glasses and serve.

YIELD: 4 SERVINGS

MENU "I CAN'T BELIEVE I MADE THIS!"

~ **SPINACH-ARTICHOKE CASSEROLE**

~ **RICE WITH SWEET RED PEPPER**

~ **SHRIMP NEWBURG**

~ **SUGGESTED DESSERT: RUM RAISIN ICE CREAM**

Spinach-Artichoke Casserole

1 pound crusty **bread** (a small round loaf)

2 boxes (10 ounces each) frozen chopped **spinach**

2 tablespoons **extra-virgin olive oil** (evoo) (eyeball it)

2 cloves **garlic**, cracked away from skin

1 can (15 ounces) quartered **artichoke hearts**, drained

1 teaspoon coarse **salt**

2 extra-large **eggs**, beaten

1/2 cup **heavy cream**

2 cups shredded **Swiss** or Gruyère cheese

1/2 cup grated **manchego** or Parmigiano Reggiano cheese

Freshly ground black **pepper**, to taste

Preheat oven to 425°F. Trim two sides of the loaf and thickly slice the bread. Place slices and ends on a baking sheet in the oven to toast.

Defrost spinach in the microwave, then squeeze dry in a clean kitchen towel.

Pour evoo into a 13-inch oval casserole dish or a 9" x 13" rectangular dish, liberally coating the sides and bottom with the oil. Rub toasted bread with cracked garlic and cut into large chunks. Reserve toasted bread ends for Shrimp Newburg, recipe follows, or for salad croutons on another night. Arrange the toasted, garlic-rubbed pieces of bread in a single layer in dish. Do not pack tightly. Add the quartered artichoke hearts to the dish, nesting them in and around the bread. Sprinkle the spinach around the casserole and season with salt. Beat eggs with cream and pour evenly over the dish. Top casserole with cheeses and pepper and bake until golden on top, 17 minutes.

YIELD: 6 SERVINGS

Rice with Sweet Red Pepper

3 cups **chicken broth**

2 tablespoons **butter**

1 & 1/2 cups white **rice**

1/2 small **red bell pepper**, finely chopped

3 tablespoons chopped fresh **parsley**, flat-leaf or curly

Bring 3 cups broth to a boil with butter. Add rice and reduce heat to simmer. Cover and cook 15 minutes, then add red pepper bits. Cook 2 to 3 minutes longer. Fluff rice with fork and combine rice mixture with parsley.

YIELD: 6 SERVINGS

Shrimp Newburg

Juice of 1 **lemon**

2 **bay leaves**

2 & 1/2 pounds large raw **shrimp**, peeled and deveined with tails removed

1 tablespoon **extra-virgin olive oil** (evoo) (once around the pan)

4 tablespoons **butter**, divided

1 large **shallot**, finely chopped

2 tablespoons **flour**

1/2 cup **chicken broth**

1 cup **heavy cream**

3 tablespoons dry **sherry**

1/4 teaspoon ground **nutmeg**

Salt and freshly ground black **pepper**, to taste

Toasted **bread** crusts or day-old baguette

1 teaspoon sweet **paprika**

2 tablespoons chopped fresh flat-leaf **parsley**

1/2 cup grated **Parmigiano** Reggiano, parmesan, or manchego (optional)

Preheat broiler to high or oven to 425°F.

Bring 3 to 4 inches of water to a boil in a large pot. Add lemon juice, bay leaves, and shrimp. Reduce heat to simmer, cover, and cook shrimp 5 minutes.

To a large skillet over medium heat add evoo, 2 tablespoons of butter and shallots. Sauté shallots 2 minutes, then add flour and cook another minute. Whisk in broth and thicken a minute. Add cream and bring to a

EARLY-BIRD 4 to 7 SPECIALS

bubble. Stir in sherry then season sauce with nutmeg, salt, and pepper. Allow sauce to reduce until thick enough to coat a spoon, about 2 to 3 minutes more. Drain shrimp and place in a shallow serving dish. Season cooked shrimp with salt.

Melt remaining 2 tablespoons butter in microwave, 15 seconds. Grate toasted or stale bread with a large box grater. Toss bread with melted butter, paprika, and parsley. Cheese may be added for a more deeply brown, saltier topping. Set aside.

Pour hot sherry sauce over shrimp. Add bread topping and toast under broiler until golden, 2 minutes or bake in hot oven, 5 minutes.

YIELD: 6 SERVINGS

It's already after seven, you need real food. Enjoy these big-flavor, low-maintenance meals designed for two. Your other half will love you even more! Or, if dining solo, make a full recipe and enjoy the leftovers for lunch.

COOKING 'ROUND THE CLOCK

SIT-DOWN
7 to 9
SUPPERS

RACHAEL RAY
30-MINUTE MEALS

MENU **RESULTS GUARANTEED**

~ **MARINATED GRILLED FLANK STEAK**

~ **BLT–SMASHED POTATOES**

~ **LEMON-BUTTER BROCCOLINI**

Marinated Grilled Flank Steak with BLT–Smashed Potatoes

2 cloves **garlic**, finely chopped

1 tablespoon **grill seasoning** blend, such as Montreal Seasoning by McCormick

1 teaspoon smoked **paprika**, ground chipotles, chili powder, or ground cumin

2 teaspoons **hot sauce**, such as Tabasco (eyeball it)

1 tablespoon **Worcestershire** sauce

2 tablespoons red wine **vinegar** (2 splashes)

1/3 cup **extra-virgin olive oil** (evoo), plus a drizzle

1 & 1/2 pounds **flank steak**

1 & 1/2 pounds small new red-skinned **potatoes**

1 **leek**, trimmed of tough tops

4 slices thick-cut smoky bacon, such as applewood-smoked **bacon**, chopped

1 small can (15 ounces) **diced tomatoes**, well-drained

1/2 cup **sour cream**, half-and-half, or chicken broth

Salt and freshly ground black **pepper**, to taste

Mix garlic, grill seasoning, paprika, hot sauce, Worcestershire sauce, vinegar, and 1/3 cup evoo in a shallow dish. Place meat in dish and coat it evenly in marinade. Let stand 15 minutes.

Meanwhile, cut larger potatoes in half; leave very small potatoes whole. Place potatoes in a small pot and cover with water. Cover pot. Bring water to a boil, remove lid, then cook potatoes until tender, 12 to 15 minutes.

Heat a grill pan or cast-iron pan over high heat.

Cut leek in half lengthwise. Chop into 1/2-inch pieces. Place leeks in a bowl of water and swish, separating the layers, to release the dirt. Drain leeks in a colander or strainer.

Grill flank steak on hot pan; 4 minutes on each side for medium rare to medium, and 6 or 7 minutes on each side for medium well.

Heat a small skillet over medium-high heat. Add a drizzle of evoo and the

bacon. Cook bacon until it begins to crisp and has rendered most of its fat, 3 to 5 minutes. Add leeks and cook until they're tender, 2 to 3 minutes. Add tomatoes and heat them through, 1 minute.

Drain potatoes and return them to the hot pot. Smash potatoes with sour cream, half-and-half, or chicken broth and the BLT: bacon, leeks, and tomatoes. Season with salt and pepper.

Remove flank steak from grill and let it sit a few minutes before slicing. Thinly slice meat on an angle, cutting against the grain. Serve sliced flank steak next to BLT potatoes.

YIELD: 2 SERVINGS

Lemon-Butter Broccolini

1 pound **broccolini**
1 cup **water**
1/2 **lemon**
2 tablespoons **butter**
Salt, to taste

Trim ends from broccolini so stalks are 4 to 5 inches long. Trim a few pieces of peel off the lemon. Place broccolini in a bowl and add 1 cup water and the lemon peel. Cover the bowl with plastic wrap and microwave on high 6 minutes. Test the broccolini: It should be just tender but still bright green. Cook 2 minutes more if stems are still tough. Drain off water. Squeeze the juice from the lemon half over the broccolini and add butter and salt.

YIELD: 2 SERVINGS

MENU TURBO CLASSICS MEAL

~ GARLIC ROAST CHICKEN WITH ROSEMARY AND LEMON

~ PESTO SMASHED POTATOES

~ MIXED GREENS SALAD WITH GORGONZOLA DRESSING

Garlic Roast Chicken with Rosemary and Lemon

1 & 1/2 to 2 pounds boneless, skinless **chicken breasts,** cut into large chunks

4 cloves **garlic,** crushed

4 stems fresh **rosemary,** leaves stripped (2–3 tablespoons leaves)

3 tablespoons **extra-virgin olive oil** (evoo) (eyeball it)

Grated zest and juice of 1 **lemon**

1 tablespoon **grill seasoning** blend, such as Montreal Seasoning by McCormick, or salt and freshly ground black pepper

1/2 cup dry white **wine** or chicken broth

Preheat oven to 450°F.

Arrange chicken in a baking dish. Add garlic, rosemary, evoo, lemon zest, and grill seasoning. Toss chicken to coat, then place in oven. Roast 20 minutes. Add wine and lemon juice to the dish and combine with pan juices, then spoon over chicken. Return to oven and turn oven off. Let stand 5 minutes longer, then remove chicken from the oven. Place baking dish on trivet and serve, spooning pan juices over the chicken pieces.

YIELD: 2 SERVINGS

Pesto Smashed Potatoes

1 & 1/2 pounds small red-skinned **potatoes**

Salt, to taste

1/2 cup **chicken broth**

1/2 cup store-bought **pesto**

Cut larger potatoes in half and leave small potatoes whole. Place potatoes in a pot and cover with water; bring water to a boil. Add salt and cook until potatoes are tender, 10 to 12 minutes. Drain potatoes and return them to hot pot. Add chicken broth and smash the potatoes up. Add pesto and smash to desired consistency. Serve hot.

YIELD: 2 SERVINGS

Mixed Greens Salad with Gorgonzola Dressing

1 heart **romaine** lettuce, chopped

1 bulb **endive**, chopped

1/4 cup **walnut pieces** (a handful)

2 tablespoons red wine **vinegar**

1/4 cup **extra-virgin olive oil** (evoo) (eyeball it)

3 ounces (1/4 cup) **gorgonzola** cheese, crumbled

Salt and freshly ground black **pepper**, to taste

Combine lettuce, endive, and walnuts in a large salad bowl. Pour vinegar into a small bowl and whisk in evoo. Stir in gorgonzola. Toss salad with dressing and season with salt and pepper.

YIELD: 2 SERVINGS

MENU **RAISING THE BAR-BECUE**

~ **GREEN QUESADILLAS WITH BRIE AND HERBS**

~ **BARBECUE SAUCY SALMON ON ROMAINE SALAD WITH ORANGE VINAIGRETTE**

Green Quesadillas with Brie and Herbs

2 large (12-inch diameter) spinach **tortillas** or wraps (available on dairy aisle)

1/3 pound **brie** with herbs, sliced

2 tablespoons chopped fresh **chives** or scallions

2 tablespoons chopped fresh **tarragon** or 1 teaspoon dried tarragon

Heat a large nonstick skillet or grill pan over medium-high heat. Add a spinach wrap and warm it, 30 seconds; flip it and cover half the tortilla surface with brie and chopped chives and tarragon, using half the total ingredients. Fold tortilla over and press with a spatula. Press and cook until brie is melted and tortilla is evenly crisp and blistered on both sides, 90 seconds to 2 minutes. Repeat with remaining ingredients. Cut quesadillas into wedges and snack on them as you would cheese and crackers while you prepare the rest of the meal. (Wine would not be a bad idea either.)

YIELD: 2 QUESADILLAS

Barbecue Saucy Salmon on Romaine Salad with Orange Vinaigrette

SALMON AND BARBECUE GLAZE

1 tablespoon **extra-virgin olive oil** (evoo) (once around the pan), plus a little for drizzling

1/4 red **onion**, finely chopped

2 tablespoons red wine **vinegar**

1/2 cup **maple syrup**

1 tablespoon **tomato paste**

2 teaspoons **Worcestershire** sauce

1 teaspoon **curry powder**

2–3 drops **Liquid Smoke**

1/2 teaspoon freshly ground black **pepper**

2 fillets **salmon** or salmon steaks (6–8 ounces each)

Salt

SALAD AND DRESSING

Grated zest and juice of 1 small navel **orange**

1 clove **garlic**, finely chopped

2 teaspoons **Dijon** mustard

2 tablespoons chopped fresh **tarragon** or 1 teaspoon dried tarragon

1 teaspoon **salt**

1/4 cup **extra-virgin olive oil** (evoo) (eyeball it)

2 hearts **romaine** lettuce

3 **scallions,** chopped

Make the glaze: Heat a small saucepan over medium heat, add evoo then onion, and cook onion 3 minutes. Add vinegar and cook until reduced by half. Add syrup, tomato paste, Worcestershire, curry, Liquid Smoke, and pepper. Bring to a bubble and simmer.

Meanwhile, start the salmon: Heat a grill pan over medium-high heat. Drizzle salmon with evoo and season with salt. Grill for 3 minutes and baste liberally with the glaze. Flip salmon and glaze opposite side. If you like your salmon pink at the center, remove after another 3 minutes; for opaque salmon, grill 5 minutes on each side.

Make the salad: Whisk orange zest and juice with garlic, Dijon, tarragon, and salt, then stream in evoo, whisking to combine. Chop lettuce and toss with scallions and dressing. Pile salad onto plates and top with glazed barbecued salmon.

YIELD: 2 SERVINGS

Thicker than
soup, thinner
than stew,
stoups rule on
rainy nights!

MENU RAINY NIGHT RELIEF

~ SAUSAGE, BEANS, AND BROCCOLI RABE "STOUP"

~ ITALIAN GRILLED CHEESE AND TOMATO

Sausage, Beans, and Broccoli Rabe "Stoup"

2 tablespoons **extra-virgin olive oil** (evoo) (twice around the pan)

1 pound bulk Italian sweet **sausage**

1 medium **onion**, chopped

1 **carrot**, chopped

1 starchy Idaho **potato**, peeled and chopped into small dice

2 cloves **garlic**, chopped

1 **bay leaf**

1 can (15 ounces) **white beans**, drained

Salt and freshly ground black **pepper**, to taste

1 bunch **broccoli rabe**, chopped (3 cups)

1 quart **chicken broth**

Grated **Parmigiano** Reggiano or Romano cheese, for serving

Heat a medium pot or a deep skillet over medium-high heat. Add evoo and sausage and brown, crumbling with a spatula. Add onions, carrots, potatoes, garlic, bay leaf, and beans. Season with salt and pepper. Cook to begin to soften the vegetables, 5 minutes. Add broccoli rabe and cook just until wilted. Add chicken broth and cover pot. Raise heat and bring stoup to a boil. Reduce heat to simmer and cook 15 minutes. Remove bay leaf, adjust seasonings, and serve stoup with grated cheese for topping.

YIELD: 2 SERVINGS

Italian Grilled Cheese and Tomato

2 tablespoons extra-virgin olive oil (evoo) (twice around the pan)
1 large clove garlic
4 slices crusty Italian bread
6 deli slices provolone cheese
1 vine-ripened tomato, cut into 6 slices
Salt and freshly ground black **pepper, to taste**
8 fresh basil leaves, torn

Heat a large griddle or large nonstick skillet over medium heat. Add evoo and garlic and cook 1 minute. Add bread to the pan to soak up garlic oil. Top each slice of bread with 1 & 1/2 slices provolone each. Add 3 tomato slices to each of 2 slices of bread and season with salt and pepper. Top tomatoes with lots of basil. Set the other two slices of bread on top of the basil to form sandwiches. Cook grilled cheeses until golden brown and cheese has melted, flipping and pressing with a spatula. Cut from corner to corner and serve.

YIELD: 2 SERVINGS

MENU NOW AND THEN

~ **RETRO-METRO FANCY TUNA CASSEROLE**

~ **ICEBERG LETTUCE SALAD WITH TANGY TOMATO-TARRAGON "FRENCH" DRESSING**

Retro-Metro Fancy Tuna Casserole

1/4 loaf day-old crusty **bread** or 1 day-old crusty roll

Salt and freshly ground black **pepper**, to taste

1/2 pound extra-wide egg **noodles** or 1 box (12 ounces) egg fettuccini

1 pound **tuna** steak

1 cup white **wine**

1 **bay leaf**

A few whole **peppercorns**

1 tablespoon **extra-virgin olive oil** (evoo) (once around the pan)

4 tablespoons **butter**

1 large **shallot**, chopped

8–10 white **mushrooms**, thinly sliced

1 teaspoon ground **thyme** or poultry seasoning

2 tablespoons all-purpose **flour**

1 & 1/2 cups **chicken broth**

1/2 cup **heavy cream** or half-and-half

1/2 cup baby frozen **peas**

Chopped fresh flat-leaf **parsley**, for garnish

Place bread in toaster oven on medium heat to dry and toast, 20 minutes. Bring a large pot of water to a boil. Add salt, then pasta. Cook according to package directions to al dente (with a bite to it). Drain.

Place tuna in a small skillet and add wine; add just enough water to cover fish. Add bay leaf and peppercorns. Bring liquids to a boil. Reduce heat to simmer and cover skillet. Poach fish 12 minutes.

Meanwhile, heat a large, deep skillet over medium heat. Add evoo and 2 tablespoons of the butter. Add shallots and mushrooms and season with salt and pepper. Sauté gently 5 minutes. Sprinkle in thyme and flour and cook 1 minute, stirring with a whisk. Whisk in chicken broth, then cream. Adjust seasonings. Add peas.

Remove cooked, poached tuna to a bowl and flake fish with a fork.

Add cooked noodles and tuna to sauce. Remove sauce from heat and transfer mixture to a casserole or serving dish.

Use the biggest holes on a box grater to grate the bread into large crumbs. Melt remaining 2 tablespoons butter in a small cup in microwave and pour melted butter over bread. Scatter bread crumbs and parsley over the top of the casserole. Serve immediately.

YIELD: 2 SERVINGS, WITH A LITTLE LEFT OVER

Iceberg Lettuce Salad with Tangy Tomato-Tarragon "French" Dressing

1 small head iceberg **lettuce,** chopped

1/8 seedless **cucumber,** sliced

1/2 cup shredded **carrots** (preshredded are available in sacks in produce section)

A few cherry or grape **tomatoes**

2 tablespoons white wine **vinegar**

2 teaspoons **sugar**

1 tablespoon **tomato paste**

2 tablespoons chopped fresh **tarragon** or 2 teaspoons dried tarragon

1/4 cup **extra-virgin olive oil** (evoo) (eyeball it)

Salt and freshly ground black **pepper,** to taste

Combine lettuce, cucumber, carrots, and tomatoes in a salad bowl. In a small bowl, combine vinegar and sugar, then whisk in tomato paste. Add tarragon and whisk in evoo in a slow, thin stream, then season with salt and pepper. Pour dressing over salad, toss, and serve.

YIELD: 2 SERVINGS

Clean your greens in a big bowl or a half sink full of cold water. The grit will fall to the bottom of the sink or bowl. Dry the greens on paper towels in a dish drainer board or salad spinner. Clean all greens, veggies, and herbs when you bring them home from the market. Your produce will be ready for you to use—no fuss, no mess, no wasted time.

MENU **SUPPER EXPRESS**

~ LINGUINI WITH WHITE CLAM SAUCE

~ GREENS 'N BEANS SALAD

Linguini with White Clam Sauce

Salt and freshly ground black **pepper,** to taste

1/2 pound **linguini**

1/4 cup **extra-virgin olive oil** (evoo) (eyeball it)

4–6 cloves **garlic,** finely chopped

1 tin flat **anchovy fillets** (6 or 7 fillets), drained

4 or 5 sprigs fresh **thyme,** leaves stripped (2 tablespoons),
    or 1 & 1/2 teaspoons dried thyme

1 cup dry white **wine**

1 can (15 ounces) fancy whole baby **clams** with juice

Grated zest of 1 **lemon**

2 tablespoons chopped **parsley**

Crusty **bread,** to pass at table

Put a large pot of water over high heat. When water boils, add salt and pasta. Cook pasta until slightly underdone, 6 to 7 minutes.

Meanwhile, heat a large, deep skillet over medium heat. Add evoo, garlic, and anchovies and cook until anchovies have melted into evoo. Add thyme and wine. Simmer wine to reduce, 1 minute. Stir in clams with their juice and the lemon zest.

Drain pasta and add to skillet and toss with sauce; cook 2 to 3 minutes, until pasta is al dente and has absorbed some of the sauce and flavor. Add parsley, salt, and pepper and serve with bread for mopping up remaining juices.

YIELD: 2 SERVINGS

Greens 'n Beans Salad

1/2 head **escarole,** chopped
1/2 head green or red leaf **lettuce,** chopped
1 can (15 ounces) **cannellini,** drained
1/4 red **onion,** chopped
1 clove **garlic,** minced
1 teaspoon **sugar**
1 tablespoon **lemon** juice
1 tablespoon red wine **vinegar**
3 tablespoons **extra-virgin olive oil** (evoo)
Salt and freshly ground black **pepper,** to taste

Arrange greens on a large platter or in a salad bowl. Top with beans and
red onions.

Make the dressing: In a small bowl, blender, or food processor combine
garlic, sugar, lemon juice, and vinegar. Whisk in evoo. Pour dressing
evenly over the salad. Season salad with salt and pepper, toss, and serve.

YIELD: 2 SERVINGS

MENU **FUN-YET-FIT FOOD**

~ **BLACKENED CHICKEN PIZZA WITH YELLOW TOMATO SALSA**

~ **CHOPPED SALAD WITH LOW-FAT RANCH DRESSING**

~ **SORBET SHAKES**

Blackened Chicken Pizza with Yellow Tomato Salsa

1 tablespoon **grill seasoning** blend, such as Montreal Seasoning by McCormick

1 teaspoon sweet **paprika** (eyeball it)

1 teaspoon **chili powder**

1/2 teaspoon **cayenne** pepper or a few drops hot sauce, such as Tabasco

1/2 to 3/4 pound **chicken breast**, sliced thin

1 tablespoon vegetable **oil** (once around the pan)

All-purpose **flour** or corn meal, for dusting

1 store-bought **pizza dough**

1/2 pound brick reduced-fat cheddar **cheese with jalapeño** or chipotle pepper, such as Cabot brand

2 small **yellow tomatoes**, seeded and chopped

1/4 cup chopped red **onion**

1 **jalapeño** pepper, seeded and finely chopped

2 tablespoons **cilantro** (optional)

2 tablespoons fresh **thyme** leaves

1 clove **garlic**, cracked away from skins

Salt, to taste

Grated zest and juice of 1/2 **lime**

Preheat oven to 450°F.

Heat a large, heavy skillet over very high heat. Combine grill seasoning, paprika, chili powder, and cayenne pepper on a plate. Press chicken slices into seasoning on one side. Add oil to screaming hot pan and cook chicken 2 minutes on each side. Remove chicken from skillet and chop.

Sprinkle a little flour or corn meal on a pizza pan or cookie sheet and stretch out pizza dough on pan. Shred reduced-fat cheese.

Make the salsa: Combine tomatoes, onion, jalapeño, cilantro (if using), and thyme. Make a garlic paste by chopping garlic then adding a generous pinch of salt and mashing it together with the flat of the knife. Add garlic paste to salsa. Add lime zest and juice and mix salsa well.

Scatter chicken, salsa, and cheese over pizza dough, working to the edges. Bake until crisp and bubbly-brown on top, 12 to 15 minutes.

YIELD: 2 SERVINGS

Chopped Salad with Low-Fat Ranch Dressing

1 sack (10 ounces) mixed **greens**

1/2 cup shredded **carrots** (preshredded are available in produce section)

3 **radishes**, sliced

1 cup plain low-fat **yogurt**

2 tablespoons grated or finely chopped **onion**

2 tablespoons chopped fresh flat-leaf **parsley**

2 tablespoons chopped or snipped fresh **dill** or 1 teaspoon dried dill

1 tablespoon fresh **lemon** juice

1 clove **garlic**

Salt and freshly ground black **pepper**, to taste

Combine greens with carrots and radishes in a large salad bowl.

Make the dressing: Mix yogurt with onion, parsley, dill, and lemon juice. Make a garlic paste by chopping garlic then adding a generous pinch of salt and mashing it together with the side of the knife. Mix paste into dressing. Season the dressing with pepper. Pour dressing evenly over salad, toss, and serve.

YIELD: 2 SERVINGS

Sorbet Shakes

1 pint chocolate **sorbet** or strawberry sorbet

2 cups **skim milk**

Cool Whip or other nondairy low-fat topping

If sorbet is too firm to scoop, soften in microwave for 10 seconds on high. Blend milk and sorbet in blender on high and pour into 12-ounce tumblers. Top shakes with whipped topping.

YIELD: 2 SHAKES

MENU ONE-POT DINNER, ONE-DISH DESSERT

~ CHICKEN, CHORIZO, AND TORTILLA "STOUP"

~ PECAN PIE SUNDAES

Chicken, Chorizo, and Tortilla "Stoup"

3/4 pound **chicken tenders**

Salt and freshly ground black **pepper**, to taste

1/2 pound **chorizo** sausage (available in packaged meats section)

2 tablespoons **extra-virgin olive oil** (evoo) (twice around the pan)

2 cloves **garlic**, smashed

1 small **red bell pepper**, chopped

1 small **onion**, chopped

4 small red-skinned **potatoes**, diced

1 can (15 ounces) dark red **kidney beans**, drained

2 teaspoons **hot sauce**, such as Tabasco

1 can (15 ounces) chopped **fire-roasted tomatoes**, such as Muir Glen brand

1 quart **chicken broth**

1 sack red or blue corn **tortilla chips**, any size or flavor, crushed

2 cups shredded **pepper-Jack** or smoked cheddar cheese

Chopped **scallions**, for garnish (optional)

Chopped **cilantro**, for garnish (optional)

Fresh **thyme**, for garnish (optional)

Chop tenders into bite-size pieces. Wash up, then season chicken with salt and pepper. Dice chorizo. Heat a medium soup pot over medium-high heat. Add evoo and chicken to pot. Lightly brown chicken 2 minutes, then add chorizo and garlic. Cook another 2 to 3 minutes, then add peppers, onions, and potatoes. Cook 5 minutes, then stir in beans, hot sauce, and tomatoes. Add chicken broth and bring stoup to a bubble. Reduce heat and simmer until potatoes are tender, 10 to 12 minutes. Preheat the broiler. Ladle stoup into shallow bowls and top each bowl with a generous handful of crushed tortilla chips and cheese. Melt cheese under hot broiler. Garnish with scallions and herbs, if desired.

YIELD: 2 SERVINGS (WITH SECONDS)

Pecan Pie Sundaes

1 cup crushed cinnamon **graham crackers**
1/2 cup store-bought **caramel dessert sauce**
1 pint butter pecan **ice cream**
1 canister **whipped cream**
1 sack (2 ounces) chopped **pecans** (available in baking section)
2 **maraschino cherries** (optional—but more fun)

Put a handful of graham cracker crumbs into a goblet or sundae bowl. Heat caramel sauce in microwave oven on high for 1 minute.

Top graham cracker crumbs with a scoop of ice cream then add more crumbs, caramel sauce, another scoop of ice cream, and more caramel sauce. Top with whipped cream, tons of chopped pecans, and a cherry.

YIELD: 2 BIG SUNDAES

MENU **GOURMET GUT-BUSTER BURGER**

~ ITALIAN SLAW SALAD

~ GORGONZOLA AND SAGE SIRLOIN BURGERS

Italian Slaw Salad

3 tablespoons fresh **lemon juice**

1 tablespoon **sugar**

1 teaspoon **poppy seeds**

1/4 to 1/3 cup **extra-virgin olive oil** (evoo)

2 heads **radicchio**, shredded

1/4 Savoy **cabbage**, shredded, or 1 romaine heart, shredded

1 tablespoon chopped fresh **dill** or 1 teaspoon dried dill

1/4 small **red onion**, finely chopped

1 can (15 ounces) cranberry, red kidney, or pinto **beans**, drained

Salt and freshly ground black **pepper**, to taste

In the bottom of a medium bowl, mix together lemon juice, sugar, and poppy seeds, then whisk in evoo. Add radicchio, cabbage, dill, onion, and beans. Toss the slaw to evenly coat it; add salt and pepper.

YIELD: 2 SERVINGS (WITH LEFTOVERS OR SECONDS)

Gorgonzola and Sage Sirloin Burgers

1 pound **ground sirloin**

1/4 cup red **wine**

2 teaspoons **Worcestershire** sauce

1 **shallot**, minced

1 large clove **garlic**, minced

4 sprigs fresh **sage**, leaves stripped and finely chopped (2 tablespoons)

1 tablespoon **grill seasoning** blend, such as Montreal Seasoning by McCormick

Extra-virgin olive oil (evoo), for drizzling

1/4 to 1/3 pound **gorgonzola** cheese, crumbled

2 crusty onion Kaiser **rolls**, split

Red leaf **lettuce**

Sliced **tomato**

Terra brand red bliss, sun-dried tomato, and herb chips or Yukon gold onion and garlic **chips**

Heat a nonstick skillet over medium-high to high heat. Mix beef in a bowl with wine, Worcestershire, shallot, garlic, sage, and grill seasoning, and form 2 BIG patties, 1 to 1 & 1/2 inches thick. Drizzle burgers with evoo and place on hot skillet. Cook 5 or 6 minutes, then flip. Top burgers with big mounds of cheese and loosely cover the skillet with aluminum foil. Cook until burger is cooked through and cheese has melted, 3 or 4 minutes.

Place burgers on bun bottoms and leave open-faced, with the tomato and lettuce on the bun tops. Top and assemble burgers when you sit down to eat. Pile some chips alongside each burger and mound up some slaw salad, then open REALLY wide and dig in!

YIELD: 2 SERVINGS

MENU **EXOTIC BURGERS**

~ **TURKEY TIKKA BURGERS**

~ **INDIAN CORN**

Turkey Tikka Burgers with Indian Corn

Since ground turkey comes preportioned in a package, this recipe will yield three burgers. To reheat the leftover burger, microwave it on high for two and a half minutes. Also, you can chop cold leftover burger and add it to a tossed salad for a quick lunch. Sprinkle in some sliced almonds for added flavor.

INDIAN CORN

2 large ears **corn** on the cob, husked

2 tablespoons **butter**

1 teaspoon **chili powder**

1 teaspoon **cumin**

1/2 teaspoon **turmeric**

1/4 teaspoon **cardamom**

Salt, to taste

BURGERS

1 package (about 1 & 1/4 pounds) ground **turkey breast**

2 **scallions**, chopped

2 inches **gingerroot**, peeled and grated or chopped

2 cloves **garlic**, chopped

1/4 small **red bell pepper**, chopped (3 tablespoons)

2 tablespoons chopped fresh **cilantro**

1 rounded tablespoon mild **curry paste** (available on international foods aisle)

1 tablespoon **grill seasoning** blend, such as Montreal Seasoning by McCormick

1/2 cup plain **yogurt**

Vegetable or olive **oil** for drizzling

2 large Kaiser **rolls**, split

1 jar (8 ounces) mango **chutney** (available on condiment aisle)

4 pieces red-leaf **lettuce**, for topping

1/2 vine-ripened **tomato**, sliced

1 chunk (3 inches) seedless **cucumber**, stood on end then thinly sliced into strips

Start the corn: Set corn in a skillet and cover with water. Bring to a boil and cook corn 5 minutes. Drain and return to pan.

While corn is cooking, make the burgers: Heat a large nonstick skillet over medium-high heat. Mix turkey with scallions, ginger, garlic, bell pepper, cilantro, curry paste, grill seasoning, and yogurt. Form 3 large patties and drizzle patties with oil. Cook in hot skillet 5 minutes on each side.

Back to the corn: Melt butter with chili powder, cumin, turmeric, cardamom, and salt in microwave on high for 10 seconds. Stir melted butter and spices to combine then pour over hot corn in pan. Shake pan to roll corn evenly in butter and spices.

Place burgers on bun bottoms. Spread mango chutney on bun tops. Top burgers with lettuce and tomato and sliced cucumber and set bun tops in place. Serve with spiced corn on the cob on the side.

YIELD: 2 SERVINGS (PLUS 1 LEFTOVER PATTY)

ONE-HOT-POT

Chili Verde

2 tablespoons vegetable, sunflower, or corn **oil** (twice around the pan)

1 & 1/3 pounds ground **turkey breast** or chicken breast

2 & 1/2 tablespoons ground **cumin** (a generous palmful)

2 tablespoons **hot sauce**, such as Tabasco

1 & 1/2 tablespoons **grill seasoning** blend, such as Montreal Seasoning by McCormick

1 **jalapeño**, seeded and chopped

3 cloves **garlic**, chopped

1 small white **onion**, chopped

1 small **zucchini**

1 small yellow or green **bell pepper**, seeded

12 **tomatillos**, husks removed

2–3 tablespoons chopped **cilantro** leaves (a handful)

1 & 1/2 tablespoons fresh **thyme** leaves or 1 teaspoon dried thyme

1 can (15 ounces) **pinto beans**, drained well

Shredded **cheddar**, Monterey Jack, pepper-Jack, or smoked cheddar cheese, for topping chili (optional)

2 **scallions**, chopped

Corn chips, polenta chips, or soy chips, for dipping and scooping (optional)

Heat a deep skillet over medium-high heat. Add oil and turkey. Season turkey with cumin, hot sauce, and grill seasoning. Start to brown and crumble the turkey and add jalapeño, garlic, and onion to the pan. Chop and add zucchini and bell peppers as you work: chop and drop into the pan. Let the vegetables and turkey cook while you chop tomatillos. Stir in tomatillos; add cilantro, thyme, and beans, then cover the pot. Reduce heat to medium. Cook 5 minutes, covered; remove the lid and cook another 3 to 5 minutes. Adjust seasonings.

Ladle chili verde into bowls. Top with cheese, if using, and chopped scallions. Serve with chips of choice for dipping, if desired.

YIELD: 2 SERVINGS (WITH LEFTOVERS OR BIG SECONDS)

15-MINUTE MEAL—FOR REAL

Vicki's Chicken and Grapes with Creamy Mustard Sauce and Couscous

Vicki Cusimano makes this for her husband Andy. They have been married 40 years and are sickeningly in love. I am going to keep making this for my fiancé, John. He's their son. I hope it brings me 40 more happy years, too—and many more!

3 tablespooons all-purpose **flour**

1 tablespoon **extra-virgin olive oil** (evoo) (once around the pan), plus a drizzle

2 tablespoons **butter,** cut into pieces

2 packages (1 & 1/4 to 1 & 1/2 pounds total) **chicken tenders**

Salt and freshly ground black **pepper**

1/3 cup white **wine** (eyeball it)

1 cup **half-and-half**

1/4 cup grainy stone-ground **mustard**

1 cup seedless red **grapes,** halved

2 cups **chicken broth**

2 cups **couscous**

Place flour in a shallow bowl. Place a large skillet over medium to medium-high heat; add 1 tablespoon evoo and the butter. Dredge chicken in flour; season with salt and pepper. Add chicken to skillet and cook until browned, 7 or 8 minutes. Add wine and scrape up browned bits as wine comes to a bubble; cook the liquid down, 30 seconds to a minute. Combine half-and-half and mustard and pour the mixture over the chicken. Add grapes to the pan and shake to coat chicken and grapes in sauce. Reduce heat to low and simmer 3 to 5 minutes more.

Meanwhile, make the couscous: Bring chicken broth and a drizzle evoo to a boil. Add couscous. Remove pan from heat and cover. Let couscous sit 5 minutes, then fluff with a fork.

Serve mounds of couscous with chicken and grapes alongside or over the top.

YIELD: 2 SERVINGS (WITH LEFTOVERS)

MAKE YOUR OWN TAKE-OUT

Honey-Cashew Chicken Salad

1 **rotisserie chicken** (available near deli section)

1/4 cup sunflower or safflower **oil** plus 3 tablespoons

4 inches **gingerroot**, peeled and thinly sliced into long matchsticks

Half a sack (3 cups) mixed **greens**

1/4 pound (1/4 of a 16-ounce sack) shredded **cabbage**

1/2 cup shredded **carrots** (preshredded are available on produce aisle)

1/4 seedless **cucumber**, thinly sliced lengthwise then cut into thin strips

2 **scallions**, chopped

A handful of **sprouts** or pea shoots, any variety

3 tablespoons **duck sauce** or plum sauce (3 take-out packets ; also available in jars on Asian foods aisle)

1 teaspoon crushed **red pepper flakes**

2 tablespoons white, rice wine, or cider **vinegar**

Salt, to taste

1 cup **honey-roasted cashews**

Remove meat from chicken and chop; reserve.

Heat 1/4 cup oil in a small skillet over medium heat. Fry ginger until crisp, 5 minutes. Remove and drain on paper towels.

Combine greens, cabbage, carrots, cucumber, scallions, and sprouts in a salad bowl. Make the dressing: Mix duck sauce or plum sauce with red pepper flakes and vinegar, then whisk in 3 tablespoons oil in a slow stream. Dress and toss salad and season with salt. Pile salad up on two large dinner plates. Top with chicken chunks, fried ginger, and lots of honey-roasted cashews.

YIELD: 2 HUGE SERVINGS

GOOD & GOOD-FOR-YOU GUT-BUSTER

Grilled Polenta and Smoked Mozzarella Caprese

This dinner tastes like a hearty lasagna, but it's done in less than 15 minutes and is meat free!

2 tablespoons **extra-virgin olive oil** (evoo)

2 tablespoons **butter**

1 tube (24 ounces) store-bought **polenta**

Salt and freshly ground black **pepper,** to taste

2 cloves **garlic,** minced

1/4 medium **onion,** finely chopped

1/2 teaspoon crushed **red pepper flakes**

1 can (15 ounces) **fire-roasted tomatoes,** such as Muir Glen brand

1 pound **smoked mozzarella,** thinly sliced

1 cup fresh **basil** leaves

1/2 cup **sun-dried tomatoes** in oil, drained and sliced

Heat a medium nonstick skillet over medium-high heat and a small pot over medium heat and add 1 tablespoon evoo to each. To the skillet, add butter and let it melt into oil. Slice polenta into 3/4-inch slices and add to skillet then season with salt and pepper. To the small pot, add garlic, onions, and crushed pepper and cook 3 to 5 minutes, then add tomatoes, season with salt and pepper, and simmer 5 minutes more.

Cook polenta slices until golden brown and crisp, 3 or 4 minutes on each side. Place polenta disks on a platter and layer with thinly sliced mozzarella, basil leaves, and sun-dried tomatoes. Pour tomato sauce across and over the layered polenta and cheese and serve immediately.

YIELD: 2 SERVINGS

MENU GO FISH!

~ SWORDFISH KEBABS

~ TOMATO, ONION, AND ARUGULA SALAD

Swordfish Kebabs with Tomato, Onion, and Arugula Salad

1 & 1/2 pounds **swordfish** steak

Grated zest of 1 **lemon**

A handful of fresh flat-leaf **parsley** leaves

1 large clove **garlic**

1 teaspoon **salt**

Extra-virgin olive oil (evoo), for drizzling

3 small vine-ripened **tomatoes**, seeded and chopped

1/2 cup chopped white **onion**

2 cups **arugula**, chopped

Freshly ground black **pepper**, to taste

Lemon wedges, for serving

Preheat broiler.

Cube swordfish into 1-inch pieces and thread onto 2 metal skewers. Pile lemon zest with parsley and garlic and chop together. Add salt and rub it into the mixture with the flat of the knife, forming a paste. Drizzle fish with evoo and rub the paste evenly over kebabs. Place kebabs on broiler pan and broil on top rack until fish is firm and opaque, about 3 minutes on each side.

Make the salad: Mix tomatoes, onions, and arugula together. Drizzle with evoo and season with salt and pepper. Place half the salad on each of 2 plates. Top with a skewer of fish and serve with wedges of lemon.

YIELD: 2 SERVINGS

Armchair eats for at-home fans.
These are serious, throw-down,
mega-munchies for movie or sports
watching. Each recipe can be easily
adjusted to serve one or more. Let
the flicks roll and the games begin!

COOKING 'ROUND THE CLOCK

TV DINNERS 7 to 12 & SNACKS

RACHAEL RAY 30-MINUTE MEALS

MENU GET YOUR GAME ON!

~ CHILI DOG NACHOS
~ BUFFALO CHICKEN SALAD

Chili Dog Nachos

1 tablespoon vegetable **oil** (once around the pan)

1 pound **ground sirloin**

Salt and freshly ground black **pepper**, to taste

3 **hot dogs**, sliced into 1/2-inch pieces

1 medium **onion**

2 teaspoons **Worcestershire** sauce

2 tablespoons **chili powder**

2 teaspoons **cumin** (half a palmful)

1 can (8 ounces) **tomato sauce**

1 sack yellow-corn **tortilla chips**, any size

1 sack (10 ounces) preshredded yellow **cheddar** cheese
    (available on dairy aisle)

Heat a medium skillet over high heat. Add oil then beef. Begin to brown and crumble beef with a wooden spoon, 2 minutes, seasoning with salt and pepper. Add chopped hot dogs and continue browning, another 3 minutes. Chop 3/4 of the onion for the chili, and finely chop the remaining 1/4 part of onion to use later as a garnish. Add chopped onions, Worcestershire, chili powder, and cumin. Mix well. Add tomato sauce and simmer chili 8 to 10 minutes over low heat. If chili gets too thick, add a splash of water.

Preheat the broiler.

Arrange corn chips on a heatproof platter or in a casserole dish. Top the chips with the chili dog topping. Cover with cheese. Melt cheese under hot broiler until melted and bubbly, 2 minutes. Garnish with finely chopped raw onions and serve. Just like chili dogs!

YIELD: 4 SERVINGS

Buffalo Chicken Salad

2 hearts **romaine** lettuce, chopped

1 cup shredded **carrots** (preshredded are available in sacks on the dairy aisle)

2 ribs **celery** with greens, chopped

1/2 cup **ranch dressing**

1/2 cup crumbled **blue cheese**

1 tablespoon vegetable **oil** (once around the pan)

2 tablespoons **butter**

1 package (3/4 to 1 pound) **chicken tenders**, cut into bite-size pieces

Salt and freshly ground black **pepper**, to taste

1/4 cup **hot sauce**, such as Tabasco

Combine lettuce, carrots, and celery in a salad bowl. Combine ranch dressing and blue cheese crumbles in a small bowl.

Heat a medium skillet over medium-high heat. Add oil and butter to hot pan, then add the chicken. Season with salt and pepper and sear chicken 2 or 3 minutes, then add hot sauce. Reduce heat a little and cook until chicken is cooked through, about 5 minutes more.

Toss salad with dressing and season with salt and pepper. Top salad with chicken and serve.

YIELD: 4 SERVINGS

MENU **DESTINATION: COUCH**

~ **SUPER-STUFFED FRENCH BREAD PIZZA RUSTICA**

~ **SUN-DRIED TOMATO DIP WITH CHIPS AND VEGGIES**

Super-Stuffed French Bread Pizza Rustica

1 package (10 ounces) frozen chopped **spinach**

1 loaf (2 feet long) French **bread**

1 tablespoon **extra-virgin olive oil** (evoo) (once around the pan)

1 pound sweet Italian **sausage**

1 small **red bell pepper**, seeded and chopped

1 small **onion**, chopped

2 large cloves **garlic**, chopped

Salt and freshly ground black **pepper**, to taste

1 & 1/2 cups part-skim **ricotta** cheese

1/2 cup grated **parmesan** cheese

1/2 pound sweet **sopressata**, sliced thick from the deli, chopped

1/2 stick **pepperoni**, chopped

1 sack (10 ounces) preshredded **mozzarella** cheese

1 sack (10 ounces) preshredded **provolone** cheese

1 teaspoon dried **oregano**

1 teaspoon crushed **red pepper flakes**

Preheat oven to 425°F.

Defrost spinach in the microwave, 6 minutes on high. Wring spinach dry in a clean kitchen towel.

Split bread lengthwise and hollow it out. Cut in half across, making 4 shells for pizzas.

Heat a medium skillet over medium-high heat, add evoo, then sausage. Brown and crumble sausage using a wooden spoon. Add bell pepper, onions, and garlic. Cook 3 to 5 minutes, then add spinach. Remove mixture from heat and season with salt and pepper. Transfer to a bowl.

Combine sausage mixture with ricotta, parmesan, sopressata, and pepperoni. Fill pizzas with the mixture and top with mounded mozzarella and provolone cheeses. Place on a cookie sheet and bake until cheese melts and bubbles and bread is super crisp, 10 to 12 minutes. Top pizzas with oregano and hot pepper flakes. Serve immediately, but snack all night!

YIELD: 4 SERVINGS

Sun-Dried Tomato Dip with Chips and Veggies

3/4 pound **feta** cheese, crumbled

1/2 cup drained **sun-dried tomatoes** in oil, coarsely chopped

1 clove **garlic** or 1/2 teaspoon granulated garlic

1 teaspoon dried **thyme**

1/2 teaspoon dried **oregano**

1 cup **milk**

1 teaspoon freshly ground black **pepper**

1 sack Mediterranean-flavored **gourmet potato chips**, such as Terra brand Onion and Garlic Yukon Gold Chips

1 pound baby-cut **carrots**

1 **green bell pepper,** cut into strips

4 ribs **celery,** cut into sticks

Combine cheese, sun-dried tomatoes, garlic, thyme, oregano, milk, and black pepper in a food processor and process until smooth. Transfer to a small bowl. Serve with chips and veggies.

YIELD: 4 SERVINGS

MENU TV DINNER

~ CHICKEN CACCIATORE SUBS

~ AL FREDO'S POPCORN

Chicken Cacciatore Subs

2 tablespoons **extra-virgin olive oil** (evoo) (twice around the pan), plus more for drizzling

4 pieces (6-8 ounces each) boneless skinless **chicken breast**

Grill seasoning blend, such as Montreal Seasoning by McCormick, or salt and freshly ground black pepper

4 sub **rolls**, split

2 cloves **garlic**, cracked away from skins

1 teaspoon crushed **red pepper flakes**

2 large **portobello** mushroom caps, sliced

1 **green bell pepper**, seeded and sliced

1 large **onion**, sliced

1 teaspoon dried **oregano** (1/3 of a palmful)

Salt and freshly ground black **pepper**

1/2 cup dry red **wine** or chicken or beef broth

1 can (14 ounces) **crushed tomatoes**

2–3 tablespoons chopped fresh flat-leaf **parsley**

1/3 pound deli-sliced **provolone** cheese

Heat a grill pan or large skillet over medium to medium-high heat. Drizzle evoo on chicken, making sure it's coated, and season with grill seasoning blend or salt and pepper. Grill or pan-fry 6 minutes on each side. Set aside.

Preheat broiler. Place rolls on a cookie sheet and lightly toast them; remove, but leave the broiler on.

Heat a large skillet over medium-high heat. Add 2 tablespoons evoo, the garlic, red pepper flakes, mushrooms, bell peppers, onions, and oregano. Sauté veggies and season with salt and pepper. Cook 5 minutes, then add wine or broth. Scrape up tasty browned bits off the bottom of the pan with a wooden spoon or heat-safe spatula. Add tomatoes and parsley. Slice chicken breasts on an angle and set into sauce. Pile chicken and veggies into sub rolls and cover with sliced provolone. Place sandwiches on cookie sheet and melt cheese under hot broiler. Serve.

YIELD: 4 SERVINGS

COOKING 'ROUND THE CLOCK

Al Fredo's Popcorn

3 tablespoons vegetable **oil** (3 times around the pan)
1 cup **popping corn**
4 tablespoons (1/2 stick) **butter**
1 clove **garlic**, cracked away from skin
1 cup grated **parmesan** cheese
Salt and freshly ground black **pepper**, to taste

Place oil in a heavy pot with a lid and heat over medium-high heat. Add corn and pop, shaking the pan until popping slows to 2 or 3 seconds between pops, then remove from heat. Place butter and garlic in a microwave-safe dish and melt in the microwave, 15 seconds on high. Discard garlic clove. Pour butter over corn and sprinkle cheese over corn. Turn to coat. Season the popcorn with salt and black pepper.

YIELD: 4 SERVINGS

MENU FANCY MUNCHIES

~ PITA-SA-LA-DIP: FRENCH ONION DIP WITH PITA CHIPS

~ JUMBO SHRIMP WRAPPED WITH ARUGULA AND
   PROSCIUTTO

~ ROASTED RED PEPPER HUMMUS AND CRUDITÉS

Pita-sa-la-dip

This recipe is a knock-off of a French classic, pissaladière, a niçoise-style caramelized onion and olive tart.

2 large, sweet **onions,** coarsely chopped

2–3 tablespoons **extra-virgin olive oil** (evoo)

1 teaspoon ground **thyme** or poultry seasoning

Salt and freshly ground black **pepper,** to taste

1 tin (2 ounces) flat **anchovy fillets,** drained and chopped

1/2 cup chopped pitted **black olives,** any variety

2 containers (5 ounces each) **garlic and herb cheese,** such as
   Boursin

Chopped fresh **chives,** for garnish

2 bags **pita chips,** any size or flavor

Preheat oven to 500°F.

Toss onions with evoo, thyme, salt, and pepper. Combine with anchovies and place on a cookie sheet or other thin pan. Roast 20 minutes, turning once. Transfer onions to a food processor, and process with olives and cheese until smooth. Adjust seasonings, transfer to a bowl, and garnish with lots of chopped chives. Surround dip with pita chips and serve.

YIELD: 2 & 1/2 CUPS

Jumbo Shrimp Wrapped with Arugula and Prosciutto

16 cooked jumbo **shrimp**

Grated zest and juice of 1 **lemon**

2 cloves **garlic,** finely chopped

Salt and freshly ground black **pepper,** to taste

2 tablespoons **extra-virgin olive oil** (evoo) (eyeball it)

1 cup **arugula** leaves, trimmed

8 slices (1/4 pound) imported **prosciutto,** cut in half

16 grape **tomatoes**

16 **toothpicks**

Place shrimp in shallow dish and add lemon zest and juice, garlic, salt, pepper, and evoo. Toss shrimp to coat evenly with dressing. To assemble, place a shrimp on 2 or 3 arugula leaves then wrap arugula around the shrimp using a piece of prosciutto on the very outside. Nest a grape tomato into the curve of the prosciutto-wrapped shrimp and secure into place with a toothpick. Repeat to wrap all the shrimp.

YIELD: 16 JUMBO SHRIMP

Roasted Red Pepper Hummus and Crudités

Many brands of hummus offer a roasted red pepper variety, but taking five minutes to dress up a plain hummus will result in a much richer dip, with the added flavor of extra lemon juice and garlic, and the colorful appeal of additional red peppers.

1 jar (14–18 ounces) **roasted red peppers**, drained

2 tablespoons fresh **lemon** juice

1 clove **garlic**, cracked away from skin

1 & 1/2 cups store-bought **hummus**, such as Tribe of Two Sheiks brand 40-Spice Hummus

Chopped **parsley**, for garnish

1 teaspoon crushed **red pepper flakes**, for garnish

1 medium **zucchini** or 1/2 seedless European cucumber, sliced into 1/4-inch disks

1/2 pound store-bought cut **carrot** sticks

6 ribs **celery** and their greens, halved lengthwise, then cut into 3- to 4-inch sticks

Coarsely chop peppers and place them in a food processor with lemon juice and garlic. Pulse-grind peppers to get them going, then scrape in hummus and process until dip is smooth and evenly red in color. Transfer dip to a bowl and garnish with parsley and crushed pepper flakes. Place bowl on a platter and arrange zucchini or cucumber, carrot sticks, and celery sticks around the dip.

YIELD: 6 TO 8 SERVINGS

MENU MANCHURIAN MUNCHIES

~ ASIAN-GLAZED WINGS

~ SESAME 5-SPICE ROASTED NUTS

~ WARM BRIE WITH FUJI APPLE, PEAR, AND MELBA ROUNDS

Asian-Glazed Wings

2 tablespoons vegetable or olive **oil** (twice around the pan)

12 whole **chicken wings** (drummers and tips)

Salt and freshly ground black **pepper**

3/4 cup **plum sauce** (available on Asian foods aisle)

1/2 cup **orange juice** (eyeball it)

2 inches **gingerroot**, peeled

3 tablespoons **tamari** (dark soy sauce) (eyeball it)

1/2 to 1 teaspoon crushed **red pepper flakes**, medium hot to extra spicy

1/4 cup chopped fresh **cilantro** leaves

1/4 cup chopped fresh **basil** leaves

Preheat oven 400°F.

Heat a large ovenproof skillet over high heat with the oil. (If you don't have an ovenproof skillet, wrap the handle twice tightly with aluminum foil.) Liberally season chicken wings with salt and pepper. When the skillet is screaming hot, add wings in one even layer. Brown wings 3 minutes per side.

Make the glaze: In a small pot over high heat combine plum sauce, orange juice, ginger, tamari, and pepper flakes. Bring up to a simmer then lower the heat to warm, reserving sauce until the wings are done browning. Remove ginger from glaze. Pour the glaze over the browned wings. Place the skillet in the oven and roast 20 minutes, flipping the wings once halfway through.

Remove the wings from the oven, if the glaze is not syrupy and thick, place the skillet on the stove and turn the heat on high, allow the glaze to reduce for about 1 minute. Toss the wings around in the glaze and finish with the fresh cilantro and basil. Serve hot or at room temperature.

YIELD: 4 SERVINGS

Sesame 5-Spice Roasted Nuts

1 cup peeled whole **almonds** (available in bulk foods section)

1 cup whole peeled **hazelnuts** (available in bulk foods section)

2 tablespoons **sesame seeds**

2 tablespoons **butter**

2 teaspoons Chinese **5-spice powder** (ground star anise, Szechuan peppercorn, cinnamon, cloves, fennel seed) (available on spice aisle)

1 tablespoon **hot sauce**, such as Tabasco

1 cup **smoked almonds**, such as Diamond brand (available on snack aisle)

Preheat oven or toaster oven to 400°F. Roast almonds and hazelnuts 7 to 8 minutes (your nose will know when they're done).

Toast sesame seeds over medium heat in a small skillet, 2 minutes; remove and reserve. Add butter to the empty skillet and let it melt. Add 5-spice powder and hot sauce. Add roasted nuts and smoked nuts and toss to coat in butter. Add sesame seeds and toss with nuts. Transfer to a small bowl and serve warm.

YIELD: 3 CUPS

Warm Brie with Fuji Apple, Pear, and Melba Rounds

1 large Fuji **apple**

1 large red- or brown-skinned **pear**, slightly underripe

A wedge of **lemon**

1 wheel (1 pound) **brie** cheese

24 sesame **Melba toast** rounds, any brand

Quarter apple and pear lengthwise and cut into each quarter on an angle to remove the core. Slice apple and pear into 1/4-inch-thick slices. Squeeze a little lemon juice over the fruit to slow browning.

Cut the top rind off the brie and place it on a microwave-safe plate. Microwave on high, 60 seconds. If brie is not yet soft and hot after 1 minute, place it back in microwave for another 30 seconds on high.

Serve warm brie with a platter of fruit and Melba toasts for dipping and spreading. Reheat for 20 to 30 seconds at a time on high if the brie "tightens" up.

YIELD: 4 SERVINGS

MENU MAKE YOUR OWN TAKE-OUT

~ HOT AND COLD SESAME NOODLES

~ THAI-GLAZED-CHICKEN LETTUCE WRAPS

Hot and Cold Sesame Noodles

Salt, to taste

1/2 pound **spaghetti**

1/4 cup **tamari** (dark soy sauce) (eyeball it)

1/4 cup (3 rounded tablespoons) smooth **peanut butter,** softened in microwave 15 seconds on high

2 tablespoons cider **vinegar** or rice wine vinegar

2–3 tablespoons **hot sauce**

1 tablespoon **dark sesame oil** (eyeball it)

2 cups shredded **cabbage and carrot mix** (available in produce department)

1 cup **bean sprouts** or pea shoots, any variety (available in produce department)

3 **scallions,** chopped on an angle

2 tablespoons **sesame seeds**

Place a large pot of water over high heat to boil. Add salt, then pasta. Cook to al dente (with a bite to it), then cold-shock to stop the cooking process by running pasta under cold water in a colander. Drain the pasta very well.

To a large bowl add tamari and the softened peanut butter. Whisk together until peanut butter and tamari are totally incorporated. Add the vinegar, hot sauce, and sesame oil and whisk into sauce. Add noodles, cabbage and carrots, sprouts, and scallions and toss to combine and coat evenly with sauce. Sprinkle sesame seeds throughout the salad and serve.

YIELD: 4 SERVINGS

COOKING 'ROUND THE CLOCK

Thai-Glazed-Chicken Lettuce Wraps

1 pound thin-cut **chicken breast** meat (available packaged in meat case)

Grill seasoning blend, such as Montreal Seasoning by McCormick

2 tablespoons vegetable **oil** (twice around the pan)

2 teaspoons **hot chili oil** or 1 teaspoon crushed hot red pepper flakes

2 tablespoons minced fresh **gingerroot**

4 cloves **garlic**, minced

1 large **red bell pepper**, seeded and very thinly sliced

1 cup shredded **cabbage**

3 **scallions**, chopped on an angle

1/2 cup **plum sauce** or duck sauce (available on Asian foods aisle)

2 cups loosely packed **basil** leaves

1 tablespoon **fish sauce** (available on Asian foods aisle) (optional)

1/3 seedless **cucumber**, chopped

1 small head iceberg **lettuce**, quartered

Thinly slice chicken into strips and sprinkle with grill seasoning.

Heat a large skillet to screaming hot. Add vegetable oil and chicken. Cook chicken 2 minutes, stirring constantly. Add chili oil or pepper flakes, ginger, garlic, bell peppers, cabbage, and scallions and stir-fry another 2 minutes. Add plum sauce and toss 1 minute, then add basil and wilt leaves into dish. Add fish sauce (if using) and turn to coat.

Transfer cooked chicken and vegetables to a bowl and serve alongside chopped cucumber for topping and cut lettuce, for wrapping. Place spoonfuls of chicken into a piece of lettuce with cucumber and fold lettuce over to eat—like small tacos.

YIELD: 4 SERVINGS

Enjoy this menu with your favorite TV season finales: It's good, healthy, fun food that's all wrapped up! For dessert serve fortune cookies (because who knows what the future holds, until next season!) and green tea ice cream.

MENU IT'S A WRAP! PARTY

~ **BACON-WRAPPED SHRIMP AND SCALLOPS**

~ **CHINESE-BARBECUED-CHICKEN LETTUCE WRAPS**

~ **CHINESE 5-SPICE POPCORN**

Bacon-Wrapped Shrimp and Scallops

12 jumbo **shrimp** (16–20 count per pound), raw, peeled and deveined

12 large sea **scallops**, trimmed and well drained

Grated zest and juice of 1 **lime**

1 tablespoon toasted **sesame oil**

1 tablespoon **grill seasoning** blend, such as Montreal Seasoning by McCormick, or coarse salt and freshly ground black pepper

1 teaspoon crushed **red pepper flakes**

12 slices center-cut or applewood-smoked **bacon**, cut in half

Toothpicks

3 **scallions**, very thinly sliced on an angle

Preheat oven to 425°F.

Place shrimp and scallops in a shallow dish or bowl. Dress seafood with lime zest and juice, sesame oil, grill seasoning blend, and red pepper flakes. Wrap each shrimp and scallop in a half-slice of bacon. Wrap each shrimp working from head to tail, pulling bacon snugly around the shrimp. Wrap the bacon around the outside of each scallop. Fasten bacon in place as necessary with toothpicks.

Arrange shrimp and scallops on a slotted baking pan, such as a broiler pan, to allow draining while bacon crisps. Bake shrimp and scallops until shrimp is pink and curled, scallops are opaque, and bacon is crisp, 10 to 14 minutes (shrimp may finish before the scallops).

Arrange cooked seafood on platter and sprinkle with chopped scallions.

YIELD: 4 SERVINGS

Chinese-Barbecued-Chicken Lettuce Wraps

2 cups fresh shiitake **mushrooms** (4 handfuls)

1 & 1/3 to 1 & 1/2 pounds thin-cut **chicken breast** or chicken tenders

2 tablespoons vegetable **oil** or peanut oil (twice around the pan)

Salt and freshly ground black **pepper**, to taste

3 cloves **garlic**, chopped

1 inch **gingerroot**, finely chopped or grated (optional)

Grated zest of 1 **orange**

1/2 **red bell pepper**, diced small

1 small tin (6–8 ounces) sliced **water chestnuts**, drained and chopped

3 **scallions**, chopped

3 tablespoons **hoisin** sauce (Chinese barbecue sauce) (available on Asian foods aisle)

2 large heads iceberg **lettuce**, cores removed, heads quartered

1 navel **orange**, cut into wedges, for garnish

Remove and discard tough stems from mushrooms and brush caps with a damp towel to clean. Slice mushroom caps.

Chop chicken into small pieces.

Heat a large skillet or wok over high heat. Add oil to hot pan. Add chicken to the pan and sear meat by stir-frying a minute or 2. Add mushrooms and cook another minute or 2. Add salt and pepper, then garlic and ginger. Cook a minute more. Add orange zest then bell peppers, water chestnuts, and scallions. Stir-fry another minute. Add hoisin sauce and toss to coat the mixture evenly.

Transfer barbecued chicken to a serving platter and pile lettuce wedges alongside. Add wedged oranges to platter to garnish. To eat, pile spoonfuls into lettuce leaves, wrapping lettuce around fillings.

YIELD: 4 SERVINGS

Chinese 5-Spice Popcorn

2–3 tablespoons vegetable **oil**
1 cup popping corn
2 teaspoons Chinese **5-spice powder** (available on spice aisle)
Salt, to taste

Cover the bottom of a deep pot (with a tight-fitting lid) with a thin layer of oil and place pot over medium-high heat. Add popcorn to oil, spread in a single layer, then cover pot. Once corn begins to pop, shake pot. When popping slows, remove pan from heat. Sprinkle 5-spice powder over popped corn and season with salt.

Variations: For kettle corn with 5 spices, sprinkle extra-fine granulated sugar and salt on popped corn. For extra nutty taste and crunch, sprinkle in sesame seeds or sunflower seeds.

YIELD: 4 SERVINGS

NOT-SO-HUNGRY—JUST A SNACK

Groovy Green Goddess Dip with Veggies and Bread Sticks

1 tin (2 ounces) **anchovy fillets**, drained

1 small **shallot** (or a 2-inch piece red onion), chopped

1/2 cup fresh flat-leaf **parsley** (3 handfuls)

12 blades fresh **chives**, chopped (about 3 tablespoons)

3 sprigs **tarragon**, leaves stripped and chopped (about 2 tablespoons)

3 tablespoons white wine **vinegar** or tarragon vinegar (eyeball it)

Juice of 1/2 **lemon**

1/3 cup **extra-virgin olive oil** (evoo) (eyeball it)

1 cup **sour cream**

Freshly ground black **pepper**, to taste

1/2 pound baby-cut **carrots** (half a large sack)

4–6 ribs **celery** from the heart, cut into 4-inch sticks

1 **red bell pepper**, seeded and sliced into 1/2-inch strips

1 package **bread sticks**, any flavor or variety

Make the dip: In a food processor, combine anchovies, shallots, parsley, chives, tarragon, vinegar, and lemon juice. Turn processor on and stream in evoo. Transfer dip to a bowl and stir in sour cream and black pepper. Serve with veggies and breadsticks for dipping.

YIELD: 1 & 1/2 CUPS DIP, AND PLENTY OF DIPPERS

Serve the marinara as a dipper or topper to the stromboli and calzones.

MENU CREATURE DOUBLE FEATURE

~ **MONSTER SNACK: SPICY MEAT AND CHEESE STROMBOLI**

~ **ANOTHER MONSTER SNACK: OPEN-FACED CALZONES WITH SPINACH AND ARTICHOKES**

~ **THE BIG DIPPER: SIMPLE MARINARA DIPPING SAUCE**

Spicy Meat and Cheese Stromboli

1 tube refrigerated **pizza dough**, such as Pillsbury brand

All-purpose **flour** or cornmeal, for dusting

1/4 pound sliced **pepperoni** (about 24 slices)

6 deli slices **provolone** cheese

6 deli slices Italian **hot ham**

8 deli slices Genoa **salami**

2 tablespoons **sesame seeds**

2 teaspoons **Italian seasoning** blend

2 tablespoons grated **Parmigiano** Reggiano or Romano cheese

1 teaspoon crushed **red pepper flakes**

1 teaspoon **garlic powder**

2 tablespoons **extra-virgin olive oil** (evoo)

Preheat oven to 400°F.

Break open the tube of dough and remove dough from container. Lightly dust your hands and the dough with flour or corn meal; roll dough out onto a work surface. Stretch out dough, gently spreading out the rectangle. Cut the rectangle crosswise into 4 equal pieces (cut in half, then cut each half in half again). Cover each piece of dough with 6 slices pepperoni, 1 & 1/2 slices provolone, 1 & 1/2 slices hot ham, and 2 slices Genoa salami. Roll each piece on an angle from corner to corner making a long roll that is thicker in the middle and thinner on each end.

Mix sesame seeds, Italian seasoning, Parmigiano, red pepper flakes, and garlic powder in a small cup. Brush rolls with evoo, then sprinkle and pat seasoning mixture into the dough. Bake until evenly golden, 12 to 14 minutes, then serve.

YIELD: 4 SERVINGS

COOKING 'ROUND THE CLOCK

Open-Faced Calzones with Spinach and Artichokes

1 box (10 ounces) frozen chopped **spinach**

1 loaf **ciabatta** bread (flat, rectangular, or oval Italian bread, 12 to 14 inches long and 8 inches wide; focaccia may be substituted)

Extra-virgin olive oil (evoo), for drizzling

2 cups **ricotta** cheese

2 cloves **garlic**, chopped

3 tablespoons chopped fresh flat-leaf **parsley** (a handful)

1/4 cup grated **Parmigiano** Reggiano or Romano cheese (a generous handful)

1 can (15 ounces) **artichokes**, drained and sliced

Salt and freshly ground black **pepper**, to taste

2 cups shredded **mozzarella** cheese or Italian 4-cheese blend (preshredded is available on dairy aisle)

Preheat oven to 400°F.

Defrost spinach in the microwave, 6 minutes on high. Wring spinach dry in a clean kitchen towel.

Toast whole bread loaf on rack in oven, 5 or 6 minutes. Remove from oven and split bread in half from end to end as if it were a large sandwich roll and lay it open.

Switch oven to broiler and place rack one level from top. If your broiler is too small to place ciabatta bread under it, you can melt the cheese in oven as well (leave oven at 400°F, and see below); it simply browns faster under broiler.

Drizzle hot bread with evoo. Mix ricotta, garlic, parsley, and Parmigiano. Spread the mixture evenly over the bread halves then dot with spinach. Evenly distribute artichokes over bread; season with salt and pepper, and top with an even layer of mozzarella. Melt and brown the cheese under the broiler 3 minutes. If you are using the oven rather than broiler, the cheese will take 6 or 7 minutes to brown. Cut bread into wedges and serve.

YIELD: 4 SERVINGS

Simple Marinara Dipping Sauce

1 tablespoon **extra-virgin olive oil** (evoo) (once around the pan)
3 cloves **garlic,** finely chopped
1 teaspoon crushed **red pepper flakes**
1 tablespoon **anchovy paste** (optional, but recommended)
1 tablespoon chopped fresh flat-leaf **parsley**
1 can (15 ounces) **crushed tomatoes**
Salt and freshly ground black **pepper,** to taste

Heat a small pot over medium heat. Add evoo, garlic, pepper flakes, and anchovy paste. Stir and cook 2 minutes. Add parsley, tomatoes, salt, and pepper. Stir sauce, bring to a bubble and simmer 5 minutes over low heat then place in small bowl and serve.

YIELD: 2 CUPS

YOUR NEW FAVORITE MEAL

Pizza Salad

All-purpose **flour,** for dusting

1 store-bought **pizza dough**

1/2 cup **pizza sauce**

2 cups shredded **mozzarella** or Italian 4-cheese blend
   (preshredded is available in sacks on dairy aisle)

2 cloves **garlic,** chopped

1 teaspoon crushed **red pepper flakes**

1/3 pound **prosciutto** di Parma

3 cups **arugula** leaves

Juice of 1/2 **lemon**

Extra-virgin olive oil (evoo), for drizzling

Salt and freshly ground black **pepper,** to taste

Preheat oven to 425°F.

Sprinkle a little flour on a clean work surface. Roll or press out dough to form a 12-inch pie and place dough on a pizza pan or cookie sheet. Spread pizza sauce on dough and top with lots of cheese. Scatter garlic and red pepper flakes over the cheese. Bake pizza until cheese is bubbly and crust is crisp, about 12 minutes. Top the hot pizza with sliced prosciutto, working all the way to the crust's edge and covering the whole pie. Toss arugula with lemon juice and a little evoo. Season arugula with salt and pepper. Pile arugula up on the center of the pizza. Cut into quarters and serve.

YIELD: 2 SERVINGS

COUCH COCKTAILS

~ GINGERTAILS: GINGER ALE COCKTAILS

~ MOVIE-TINIS: ROOT BEER FLOATS FOR GROWN-UPS

Gingertails: Ginger Ale Cocktails

Lime wedges

Ice

Mount Gay spiced **rum**

Ginger ale

Add the juice of 1 lime wedge to a tall glass. Fill glass with ice. Add 2 shots spiced rum and fill glass to rim with ginger ale. Garnish glass with another wedge of lime and a straw. Repeat for more drinks.

YIELD: AS MANY AS YOU LIKE!

Movie-tinis: Root Beer Floats for Grown-Ups

Chilled martini cocktail glass

Vanilla ice cream

Vanilla vodka, such as Absolut brand, chilled

Root beer

Use a 1-ounce scoop or 2 large spoons to make a small ice cream scoop of vanilla ice cream and place it in the bottom of a cocktail glass. Add 2 shots chilled vanilla vodka and fill the glass to the rim with root beer. Repeat for more drinks.

YIELD: AS MANY AS YOU LIKE!

These meals are created to inspire "stay at home" dates. The later you serve them, the sexier the ambiance. (The dishes can wait until morning!)

COOKING 'ROUND THE CLOCK

BISTRO 9 to 12 MEALS

RACHAEL RAY 30-MINUTE MEALS

MENU **SOUTHERN COMFORT**

~ **BOURBON-ORANGE CHICKEN AND SWEET-HOT BUTTER AND BREAD**

~ **BITTERSWEET DIJON-DRESSED SALAD**

Bourbon-Orange Chicken and Sweet-Hot Butter and Bread

CHICKEN

1 tablespoon olive or vegetable **oil**

2 tablespoons **butter,** cut into small pieces

1 pound boneless, skinless **chicken breasts**

Salt and freshly ground black **pepper**

1 can (6 ounces) frozen **orange juice** concentrate

1/4 cup whole smoked or roasted and salted **almonds,** chopped

3 tablespoons **bourbon**

BUTTER AND BREAD

1 **baguette** or 3 French dinner rolls

2 tablespoons orange **marmalade**

2 tablespoons **butter**

2 teaspoons **hot sauce**

Make the Chicken: Preheat a medium to large nonstick skillet over medium-high heat. Add oil and butter. (The oil will allow the butter to come to a higher temperature without burning the milk solids in the butter.) When butter has melted and is hot, add chicken. Season with salt and pepper and brown, 3 or 4 minutes on each side. Reduce heat to medium low. Add the juice concentrate and spoon over chicken as it melts down. Simmer 5 minutes. Transfer chicken to dinner plates, leaving most of the sauce in the pan. Top chicken with the almonds.

Raise the heat on the sauce and add bourbon. Cook sauce until it is slightly browned, 2 or 3 minutes. Spoon over chicken and serve.

Make the Butter: Place bread in a warm oven or toaster oven to crisp the crust. In a small bowl, microwave the marmalade and butter 15 seconds on high. Add hot sauce and stir. Spread or brush the sweet-hot butter on the crusty, hot bread and serve alongside the chicken and salad greens.

YIELD: 2 SERVINGS

Bittersweet Dijon-Dressed Salad

1 heart **romaine** lettuce, chopped

1 bunch **watercress**, trimmed, cleaned, and chopped

2 tablespoons orange **marmalade**

1 teaspoon **Dijon** mustard

1 tablespoon red wine **vinegar**

2–3 tablespoons **extra-virgin olive oil** (evoo)

Salt and freshly ground black **pepper**, to taste

Mix the romaine and watercress in a small salad bowl. Whisk together the marmalade, mustard and vinegar, then whisk in evoo. Pour dressing over the salad and season with salt and pepper. Toss, then adjust seasonings. Mound greens alongside the bourbon chicken and serve.

YIELD: 2 SERVINGS

MENU JOHN'S FAVORITE FISH DINNER

~ HADDOCK WITH BACON, ONIONS, AND TOMATOES
~ WILTED SPINACH WITH BUTTER AND WINE

Haddock with Bacon, Onions, and Tomatoes

My sweetie and I eat a lot of fish. This is a recipe my mother first made for both of us, and I continue to make for him, as it has become a favorite!

1 pound **haddock** fillet, cut into two 8-ounce portions
1 tablespoon **lemon** juice (the juice of 1 small wedge)
Salt
Extra-virgin olive oil (evoo), for drizzling
1/2 tablespoon **butter**, softened
3 slices smoky **bacon**, chopped
3 or 4 **cippolini** (small flat-shaped Italian sweet onion), peeled and thinly sliced (a small to medium yellow onion, quartered then thinly sliced, may be substituted)
1/2 cup Italian **bread crumbs**
2–3 tablespoons chopped fresh flat-leaf **parsley** (a handful)
1 plum **tomato**, seeded and chopped

Preheat the oven to 400°F.

Rinse fish and pat dry. Sprinkle fish with lemon juice and salt. Coat an oven-safe skillet with a drizzle of evoo and the softened butter. If your skillet doesn't have an oven-safe handle, wrap it in tin foil twice and it should be fine in oven. Set fish into skillet in two portions.

Heat a small skillet over medium-high heat. Add a drizzle of evoo and the bacon. Render the bacon fat 3 minutes, then add onions. Cook onions until softened, 10 minutes. Remove pan from heat. Add bread crumbs to the pan and turn to coat them in drippings. Add parsley and combine. Top fish with coating of onions, bacon, and bread crumbs. Bake 15 minutes. Transfer fish to dinner plates, top with chopped tomato, and serve.

YIELD: 2 SERVINGS

Wilted Spinach with Butter and Wine

This dish takes only 5 minutes to prepare, so begin preheating the skillet 6 to 7 minutes before you are ready to sit down and eat.

2 tablespoons **butter,** cut into small pieces

1 sack (1 pound) triple-washed **spinach,** tough stems removed and coarsely chopped

1/2 cup dry white **wine**

Salt and freshly ground black **pepper,** to taste

Heat a medium skillet over medium heat. Melt butter into pan. Add spinach in bunches and add more to the pan as it wilts down. When all of the spinach is wilted, add wine and turn to coat. Let wine cook down a minute or two. Season with salt and pepper and serve.

YIELD: 2 SERVINGS

MENU SO-GOOD PASTA DINNER FOR 2

~ GORGONZOLA AND WALNUT SPAGHETTI

~ THREE GREENS SALAD WITH OIL AND VINEGAR

Gorgonzola and Walnut Spaghetti

Salt

1/2 to 2/3 pound **spaghetti** (a little over half of a 16-ounce box or bag)

1 tablespoon **extra-virgin olive oil** (evoo)

1 tablespoon **butter**, cut into pieces

3 cloves **garlic**, cracked away from skin, but still whole

1/2 cup chopped **walnuts**

1/2 cup **chicken broth**

1/2 cup **heavy cream**

6 ounces crumbled **gorgonzola** cheese

3 tablespoons chopped fresh **sage**, 4 sprigs

Bring a large pot of water to a boil. Add salt, then pasta. Cook to al dente, about 7 minutes.

Meanwhile, heat a large skillet over medium heat and add evoo and butter. Add garlic and nuts and cook 5 minutes. Remove the garlic when it gets golden brown. Add broth and cream and bring to a bubble. Add the cheese and melt into sauce.

Drain pasta very well and add it to the sauce. Add sage and toss to coat pasta in sauce and walnuts. Transfer to dinner plates and serve.

YIELD: 2 SERVINGS

Three Greens Salad with Oil and Vinegar

1 heart **romaine** lettuce, chopped

1 **endive**, chopped

1 cup **watercress** leaves, stems trimmed

2 tablespoons red wine **vinegar** (eyeball it)

3 tablespoons **extra-virgin olive oil** (evoo) (eyeball it)

Salt and freshly ground black **pepper**, to taste

Combine romaine, endive, and watercress in a salad bowl. Sprinkle vinegar over salad, then evoo. Toss to coat salad and season with salt and pepper. Serve salad before, during, or after pasta, as you wish.

YIELD: 2 SERVINGS

MENU CINQUE TERRA FOR 2

~ **SALAD WITH STRAWBERRIES AND BALSAMIC VINEGAR**

~ **ANCHOVY AND POTATO APPETIZERS**

~ **TUNA MARINARA WITH RAVIOLI**

This is my kind of supper. It is a meal that I shared with my true love when we were traveling in Italy. The sauce on the pasta was actually a mussel sauce, but the tuna sauce is our at-home adaptation, simpler and faster than shucking a mountain of mussels!

Salad with Strawberries and Balsamic Vinegar

1 head green leaf **lettuce**, chopped or torn

12 ripe **strawberries**, hulled and thinly sliced

3 tablespoons **balsamic vinegar**, aged for 6 or more years (available on specialty foods aisle)

3 tablespoons **extra-virgin olive oil** (evoo) (eyeball it)

Salt and freshly ground black **pepper**, to taste

Place lettuce in a salad bowl. Place sliced berries in a small bowl, cover with balsamic and let stand 15 minutes. Remove berries with a slotted spoon and add to the salad. Whisk evoo into remaining balsamic vinegar and season with salt and pepper. Dress and toss salad just before serving.

YIELD: 2 LARGE SALADS

Anchovy and Potato Appetizers

2 large fingerling **potatoes** or thin, oval-shaped white potatoes

Extra-virgin olive oil (evoo), for drizzling

Salt and freshly ground black **pepper**, to taste

4–5 tablespoons chopped **rosemary** (6 stems stripped and coarsely chopped)

1 jar (4 ounces) **anchovies** or two tins (2 ounces each), drained

2 small plum or Roma **tomatoes**, seeded and chopped

Preheat the oven to 425°F.

Slice potatoes lengthwise into thin 1/8- to 1/4-inch slices. Coat the potatoes with evoo, salt, and pepper. Top the potatoes liberally with chopped rosemary. The rosemary leaves are the bed for the anchovies. Rest 1 large anchovy or 2 small anchovies on each slice of potato: it will cover the potato slice from end to end. Top the anchovies with chopped tomato and an additional drizzle of evoo. Roast potatoes and anchovies 15 to 18 minutes, until potatoes are tender. Remove from oven and serve hot.

YIELD: 2 SERVINGS

Tuna Marinara with Ravioli

2 tablespoons **extra-virgin olive oil** (evoo) (twice around the pan)

3 cloves **garlic**, peeled and finely chopped

1 can (6 ounces) Italian **tuna** in water or oil, drained

1/4 medium **onion**, finely chopped

3–4 tablespoons chopped pitted **black olives**, such as Kalamata (available in deli section)

3–4 tablespoons finely chopped fresh flat-leaf **parsley** leaves (a handful)

1 can (15 ounces) **crushed tomatoes**

Salt and freshly ground black **pepper**, to taste

1 package (12-16 ounces) fresh **ravioli**

8–10 leaves fresh **basil**, shredded or torn

Bring a large pot of water to boil for ravioli.

Make the sauce: Heat a deep skillet over medium heat. Add evoo, then garlic. Cook garlic 1 minute, then add tuna. Break tuna up and mash it into the oil with the back of a wooden spoon. Add onions and cook 3 to 5 minutes. Add olives and parsley, and while stirring, add tomatoes. Season with a pinch of salt (if needed) and lots of pepper. Reduce heat to simmer.

Add salt to the boiling water, then and add ravioli. Cook ravioli 5 or 6 minutes, until they all float and are al dente, with a bite left to them. Drain carefully or remove the ravioli with a slotted spoon or a spider strainer.

Add cooked ravioli to sauce and turn gently, then transfer to plates. Top with remaining sauce left in the skillet and garnish with lots of basil.

YIELD: 2 SERVINGS (NO LEFTOVERS IN OUR HOUSE, BUT YOU MIGHT HAVE SOMETHING LEFT FOR LATE-NIGHT SNACKING)

MENU HOW TO SAY-YOU'RE-SORRY

~ PÂTÉ BITES AND HERB BRIE BOARD

~ CHICKEN IN TARRAGON CREAM SAUCE, WHITE AND WILD
   RICE WITH WALNUTS

~ TRIPLE CHOCOLATE PARFAITS

Pâté Bites and Herb Brie Board

Try serving this with champagne, or French or Sicilian rose wine.

2 slices **dark bread**, such as pumpernickel or German whole
   grain, lightly toasted

Whole grain **mustard**, for spreading

1/4 pound country **pâté** or mousse pâté

1/4 red **onion**, finely chopped

4 tablespoons **capers**, drained

Cornichons or baby gherkin pickles

1/3 pound herb **brie**

Water **crackers**

Red seedless **grapes**

Spread toasted bread lightly with mustard. Arrange pâté in a thin layer on
top of mustard. Top with chopped onions and capers. Cut each slice of
pâté-covered bread into 4 quarters, cutting from corner to corner. Arrange
pâté bites on a cheese board with a wedge of herb brie, served at room
temperature with crackers and small bunches of grapes.

YIELD: 2 SERVINGS

Chicken in Tarragon Cream Sauce, White and Wild Rice with Walnuts

1 package (5-7 ounces) white and wild **rice**, chicken or herb
   flavors, Uncle Ben's or Near East brands, cooked to package
   directions

2 tablespoons **extra-virgin olive oil** (evoo) (twice around the pan)

1 pound boneless, skinless **chicken breast**

Salt and freshly ground black **pepper**, to taste

1/4 cup **balsamic vinegar** (eyeball it)

1/4 cup **water** (eyeball it)

1 tablespoon **tomato paste**

1/3 cup **heavy cream** or half-and-half or 1/3 cup sour cream

3 tablespoons chopped fresh **tarragon** (4 or 5 sprigs)

1 package (2 ounces or 1/4 cup) chopped **walnuts**, available in baking section, toasted

2 tablespoons chopped fresh flat-leaf **parsley**

Start cooking rice according to package directions.

Meanwhile, heat a large skillet over medium-high heat. Add evoo, then chicken, and season with salt and pepper. Brown and cook chicken 5 minutes on each side. Transfer chicken to a plate and cover. Reduce heat a bit. Add vinegar and water; scrape up pan drippings. Stir in tomato paste, cream, half-and-half or sour cream, and tarragon. Remove skillet from heat.

Toss cooked rice with nuts and parsley. Slice chicken on an angle and arrange on a bed of rice. Top with sauce and serve.

YIELD: 2 SERVINGS (WITH A LITTLE BIT OF LEFTOVERS)

Triple Chocolate Parfaits

1/2 cup hot **fudge sauce,** any brand
2 shots **chocolate** liqueur
1/2 pint **chocolate ice cream**
1 canister of **whipped cream**
Ground **cinnamon** or cocoa powder, for garnish
Maraschino **cherries**

Heat hot fudge sauce in microwave according to package directions— remember to remove metal lid.

In two tall glasses or cocktail glasses, layer chocolate liqueur with chocolate ice cream. Top with hot fudge, whipped cream, cinnamon or cocoa powder, and cherries.

YIELD: 2 SERVINGS

MENU **TASTE OF SPRING FOR 2**

~ PRIMAVERA ORZO

~ BABY LAMB WITH ARUGULA DIPPING SAUCE

~ SUGGESTED DESSERT: SORBET, ANY FLAVOR!

Primavera Orzo

2 tablespoons **extra-virgin olive oil** (evoo)

2 cloves **garlic**, chopped

2 **shallots**, chopped

1 small **zucchini**, chopped

1 cup shredded **carrots**, chopped

1 & 1/2 teaspoons **curry** powder (half a palmful)

3 cups **chicken broth**

1 cup **orzo** pasta

1/2 cup grated **Parmigiano** Reggiano cheese

3 tablespoons chopped fresh flat-leaf **parsley** (a handful)

Salt and freshly ground black **pepper**, to taste

Heat a medium skillet over medium-high heat. Add evoo, twice around the pan in a slow stream. Add garlic, shallots, zucchini, and carrots, then sauté 5 minutes. Add curry powder and chicken broth and bring to a boil. Add orzo and bring to a boil. Cover and reduce heat to medium. Cook, stirring occasionally, until the orzo absorbs the liquid and is al dente, 10 minutes. Uncover and stir in cheese and parsley. Season with salt and pepper and serve.

YIELD: 2 SERVINGS, WITH LEFTOVERS

Baby Lamb with Arugula Dipping Sauce

2 cups **arugula,** trimmed

1/2 cup smoked **almonds**

1 **shallot,** chopped

1/2 cup **extra-virgin olive oil** (evoo), plus more for drizzling

8–10 baby **lamb chops**

Grill seasoning blend, such as Montreal Seasoning by McCormick, or salt and freshly ground black pepper

Preheat grill pan over high heat.

Make the sauce: Combine arugula, almonds, and shallots in food processor. Pulse-grind mixture. Turn processor on and stream in 1/2 cup evoo. You should end up with a thick sauce. Transfer to a small bowl.

Drizzle chops with evoo and season with grill seasoning or salt and pepper. Grill 3 minutes on each side. Transfer chops to a platter and serve with dipping sauce.

YIELD: 2 SERVINGS

MENU BIG, EASY FLAVORS

~ CHERRY TOMATO CONFIT

~ ROASTED ASPARAGUS TIPS

~ SKIRT STEAKS LACED WITH BLUE CHEESE BUTTER

Cherry Tomato Confit

2 tablespoons **extra-virgin olive oil** (evoo) (twice around the pan)

3 large cloves **garlic,** finely chopped

1 small **onion,** finely chopped

1 pint cherry **tomatoes**

2 tablespoons sherry **vinegar** or dry sherry wine

1 teaspoon **sugar**

1/2 teaspoon crushed **red pepper flakes**

Salt, to taste

Preheat oven to 375°F.

Preheat a medium skillet over medium-high heat. Add evoo, garlic, and onions. Sweat them out 2 to 3 minutes, then add cherry tomatoes. Turn tomatoes to coat in oil. Add sherry vinegar or wine, sugar, pepper flakes and salt. Toss to coat tomatoes and transfer to a baking sheet. Roast 18-20 minutes. Serve alongside steaks and asparagus.

YIELD: 2 SERVINGS

Roasted Asparagus Tips

1 pound **asparagus**, trimmed into 4- to 5-inch tips
Grated zest of 1/2 **lemon** (2 teaspoons)
1 **shallot**, finely chopped
2 tablespoons **extra-virgin olive oil** (evoo) (eyeball it)
1 teaspoon chopped dried **tarragon**
Salt and freshly ground black **pepper**, to taste
Juice of 1/4 **lemon**

Preheat oven to 375°F.

Pile asparagus onto a small baking sheet. In a small bowl, combine lemon zest, shallots, evoo, and tarragon. Pour over the asparagus spears and turn to coat. Season with salt and pepper and roast 15 minutes. Remove asparagus from oven and toss with lemon juice.

YIELD: 2 SERVINGS

Skirt Steaks Laced with Blue Cheese Butter

1 & 1/2 pounds **skirt steaks**
Extra-virgin olive oil (evoo), for drizzling
Grill seasoning blend, such as Montreal Seasoning by McCormick
3 tablespoons **butter**, softened
1/2 cup **blue cheese** crumbles
2 tablespoons **chives**, chopped

Heat a grill pan over high heat. Drizzle meat with evoo and season with grill seasoning blend. Grill meat 3 to 4 minutes on each side. Remove meat and let it rest 5 minutes to allow juices to redistribute.

Mix butter with cheese and chives.

Slice meat very thinly on an angle, place on a plate, and top with scoops of blue cheese butter. Butter and cheese will melt down over the meat. YUMMO!

YIELD: 2 SERVINGS

MENU PASSPORT TO QUEBEC

~ FRENCH ONION TARTLETS

~ CRISPY DUCK SALAD WITH BITTER ORANGE VINAIGRETTE

~ FAUX POACHED PEARS IN PORT

French Onion Tartlets

6 very thin slices white **bread** (such as Pepperidge Farm), crusts trimmed

Olive oil **cooking spray**

2 tablespoons **butter**

1 tablespoon **extra-virgin olive oil** (evoo)

1 large **onion**, very thinly sliced

1 **bay leaf**, fresh or dried

1 teaspoon ground **thyme** or poultry seasoning

Salt and freshly ground black **pepper**, to taste

1/2 pound **Swiss** cheese, shredded

Preheat the oven to 325°F.

Spray both sides of bread slices with cooking spray and press bread into a 6-cup muffin tin. If you do not own a muffin tin, disposable tins are available on the baking aisle of the market. Place bread in oven and toast until golden, 7 or 8 minutes. Remove and reserve.

Heat a medium skillet over medium to medium-high heat. Melt butter into oil. Add onions and bay leaf. Season with thyme, salt, and pepper. Cook onions until caramel-colored, 15 to 18 minutes. Discard bay leaf.

Turn broiler on.

Place spoonfuls of cooked onions in toasted bread cups. Cover onions with cheese and set tarts under hot broiler to bubble and brown the cheese. Serve with Crispy Duck Salad, recipe follows.

YIELD: 2 SERVINGS, 3 TARTS PER PERSON

Crispy Duck Salad with Bitter Orange Vinaigrette

The Bitter Orange Vinaigrette is equally delicious with grilled or sautéed chicken or pork.

1 & 1/4 to 1 & 1/2 pounds packaged **duck breast** (ask at the meat counter; it can usually be ordered for you)
4 cups mixed baby **greens**
1 head **frisée** greens (look for very light-colored frisée)
2 **scallions**, thinly sliced on an angle
1 **shallot**, finely chopped
3 tablespoons sherry **vinegar** or red wine vinegar (eyeball it)
2 tablespoons orange **marmalade**
1/3 cup **extra-virgin olive oil** (evoo) (eyeball it)
Salt and freshly ground black **pepper**, to taste
Baguette, warmed and sliced (optional)

Score fat and skin on duck breasts. Set duck breast in a large cold skillet, skin side down. Place skillet on stove and set burner to medium heat. Cook breasts 20 minutes, turning once. Meat should be pink at center.

Arrange greens on plates and top with frisée and scallions. Combine shallots, vinegar and marmalade. Let stand 10 minutes. Whisk in evoo.

Slice duck breast and arrange half of the meat on each salad. Top with dressing and garnish with onion tarts or sliced warm baguette.

YIELD: 2 SERVINGS

Faux Poached Pears in Port

1 cup **port** wine
1 **cinnamon stick**
2 whole **star anise**
1 **clove**
1 can (15 ounces) **pear halves** in syrup, reserve half of syrup
1/2 pint French **vanilla ice cream**

Place wine, cinnamon stick, anise, and clove in a pot and add pears in syrup. Heat pot over medium heat and simmer 10 to 15 minutes. Serve with French vanilla ice cream.

YIELD: 2 SERVINGS

Serve this meal with cocktails and Sinatra, Dean, or Tom Jones on the stereo.

MENU VEGAS HI-ROLLER DINNER FOR 2

~ SHRIMP DEAN MARTINIS

~ SPICY CHICKEN CIGARS

~ CLAMS CASINO ROYALE

Shrimp Dean Martinis

1 rib **celery**, finely chopped

1 rounded teaspoon prepared **horseradish**

Juice of 1/2 **lemon**

1 teaspoon **hot sauce**, such as Tabasco

1/4 cup **ketchup** or chili sauce

1/2 cup **V8** juice

Salt and freshly ground black **pepper**, to taste

12 cooked jumbo **shrimp**, peeled and deveined with tail on

1/2 **lemon**, cut into wedges

Mix the celery, horseradish, lemon juice, hot sauce, ketchup or chili sauce, and V8 together and season with salt and pepper. Pour sauce into 2 martini glasses and surround rim with 6 jumbo shrimp. Serve lemon wedges on cocktail forks alongside glasses.

YIELD: 2 SERVINGS

Spicy Chicken Cigars

1 pound ground **chicken breast**

2 teaspoons **cumin** (half a palmful)

2 teaspoons **paprika** (half a palmful)

2 teaspoons **poultry seasoning** (half a palmful)

2 teaspoons **chili powder** (half a palmful)

2 teaspoons **grill seasoning**, such as Montreal Seasoning by McCormick (half a palmful)

2 tablespoons chopped fresh flat-leaf **parsley** (a handful)

4 sheets **phyllo dough**

4 tablespoons **butter**, melted

Preheat oven to 425°F.

In a large bowl, mix chicken with spices and parsley. Place a sheet of phyllo on a nonstick cookie sheet, brush with butter, and top with a second sheet. Take half the chicken and form a 1-inch thick log the length of the

long side of the phyllo dough. Roll the log in phyllo tightly. Repeat with remaining chicken and phyllo. Cut each log into three "cigars" and brush with a dab more butter, for a total of six "cigars."

Bake 12 to 15 minutes until golden.

YIELD: 2 SERVINGS

Clams Casino Royale

Rock or pickling **salt**

12 cherrystone **clams** (buy them scrubbed), split open, and clam loosened

3 tablespoons **butter**, softened

1 small **shallot** or 1/2 large shallot, finely chopped

1 tablespoon **Old Bay seasoning** (a palmful)

1 teaspoon freshly ground black **pepper**

A few drops **hot sauce**, such as Tabasco

3 slices center-cut **bacon**, cut into 2-inch pieces

Preheat oven to 500°F.

Pour rock salt into shallow baking pan or dish and set clams upright into salt. The salt will steady them. In a small bowl, mix butter with shallots, Old Bay, pepper, and hot sauce. Dab each clam with 1 teaspoon of the mixture and top with a piece of bacon. Bake 5 to 7 minutes, until bacon is crisp and butter is brown and bubbling. YUMMO!

YIELD: 2 SERVINGS

MENU EYE FOR THE HUNGRY GUY

~ STEAK PIZZAOLA WITH THE WORKS
~ BIG MUSSELS WITH GARLIC AND DRY VERMOUTH
~ ROMAINE SALAD WITH BLUE CHEESE VINAIGRETTE

Steak Pizzaola with the Works

This is a meal that I picture ladies making for big, hard-working men on very special occasions, like a birthday, or National I-Still-Love-You-After-All-This-Time Day which falls on a different day for each of us. Serve this meal with a dry martini and pillows to rest your heads on, if you make it through eating all this! Fellas, if you have a woman with a big appetite (like me and all the women in my family), by all means, go for it! Remember the saying about the way to anyone's heart?

1 & 1/2- to 2-pound piece of porterhouse or rib-eye **steak**
Salt and freshly ground black **pepper**
3 tablespoons **extra-virgin olive oil** (evoo)
4 cloves **garlic**, cracked away from the skin
1 teaspoon crushed **red pepper flakes**
12 **mushrooms**, sliced
1 small **onion**, sliced
1 **green bell pepper**, seeded and sliced
1/3 stick **pepperoni**, casing removed, then chopped (optional)
1/2 cup dry red **wine** (eyeball it)
1 can (28 ounces) **crushed tomatoes**
1 teaspoon dried **oregano** or 2 teaspoons chopped fresh
1/4 cup grated **Parmigiano** Reggiano or Romano cheese

Heat a large nonstick skillet over high heat. Season the steak with salt and pepper. Add 2 tablespoons evoo to the pan, then steak. Brown 3 minutes on each side and remove. Add remaining teaspoon of evoo to the pan and reduce heat to medium-high. Add garlic, pepper flakes, mushrooms, onions, bell peppers, and pepperoni, if using. Cook mixture 5 minutes, then add wine and scrape up any bits from the bottom of the skillet. Add tomatoes, oregano, and salt and pepper to taste. Slide steak back in and reduce heat to medium. Cover pan and cook 5 or 6 minutes for medium rare, 10 to 12 minutes for medium well. Remove meat; cut away from bone or divide into 2 large portions. Cover steaks with sauce and top with grated cheese.

YIELD: 2 BIG GUY SERVINGS

Big Mussels with Garlic and Dry Vermouth

2 tablespoons extra-virgin olive oil (evoo) (twice around the pan)
2 cloves garlic, cracked away from skin
1 pound mussels (buy them scrubbed)
1/2 cup dry white vermouth
2 tablespoons chopped fresh flat-leaf parsley
Salt and freshly ground black pepper, to taste

Heat a medium pan over medium-high heat. Add oil and garlic, then mussels. Arrange mussels in a single layer. Add vermouth to the pan and cover. Cook until mussels open. Discard any unopened shells. Transfer mussels to a bowl. Pour juice from pan over mussels and sprinkle with parsley, salt, and pepper. Serve with a second bowl, for shells.

YIELD: 2 SERVINGS

Romaine Salad with Blue Cheese Vinaigrette

2 hearts romaine, chopped
1 clove garlic, chopped
1/2 teaspoon dried oregano
2 teaspoons sugar
2 tablespoons red wine vinegar
1/4 cup extra-virgin olive oil (evoo)
1/4 pound blue cheese crumbles (available in specialty cheese section of market)
Salt and freshly ground black pepper, to taste

Place romaine in a big bowl. In a small bowl, combine garlic, oregano, sugar, and vinegar. Add evoo to dressing in a slow stream and mix with a whisk or fork. Stir in blue cheese. Pour dressing over salad and toss. Season with salt and pepper, and serve.

YIELD: 2 BIG GUY SERVINGS

MENU **HOT HAVANA NIGHT**

~ **CUBAN-SPICED PORK TENDERLOIN AND SOFFRITO RICE**

~ **BLACK BEAN SALSA WITH EXOTIC CHIPS**

~ **SUGGESTED DRINKS AND DESSERT: TRY MOJITOS FOR TWO AND FRUIT SORBET!**

Cuban-Spiced Pork Tenderloin and Soffrito Rice

RICE

1 tablespoon olive **oil** or vegetable oil

2 slices **bacon,** chopped

1/2 medium **onion,** chopped

1/2 **green bell pepper,** chopped

1 & 3/4 cups **chicken broth**

1 cup white **rice**

2 pinches **saffron** or 1/2 teaspoon turmeric

Salt, to taste

PORK

1 package (about 1 & 1/2 pounds) small **pork tenderloins,** trimmed

4 small cloves **garlic,** cracked away from skin

2 **bay leaves** broken into halves

2 teaspoons **fennel seed** (half a palmful)

2 teaspoons ground **coriander** (half a palmful)

1 tablespoon ground **cumin** (a palmful)

Grated zest of 1 **lime**

1 tablespoon **grill seasoning** blend, such as Montreal Steak Seasoning by McCormick or salt and freshly ground black pepper

Extra-virgin olive oil (evoo) or vegetable oil, for coating

Chopped **mango** or kiwi or chopped cilantro and scallions, for garnish (optional)

Preheat oven to 450°F.

Make the rice: Heat a small pot with tight-fitting lid over medium-high heat. Add oil and bacon and brown. Add onions and peppers and sauté, 5 minutes. Meanwhile, get pork started while you have a pocket of time (see below). Return to the rice, adding broth to the pot. Bring to a boil and add rice and saffron. Cover the pot and reduce heat to simmer. Cook 15 to 18 minutes, until rice is tender.

Make the pork: Cut 4 slits into each of the loins and nest garlic and bay leaves into the meat. Place meat on nonstick baking sheet. In a small bowl, combine fennel seed, coriander, cumin, lime zest, and grill seasoning. Coat the meat with oil. Rub spices over the tenderloins and roast in oven for approximately 22 minutes.

While both the rice and pork are cooking, you can make the salsa (recipe follows).

Remove the tenderloins from the oven. Let pork juices redistribute, then slice and serve with soffrito rice and if you wish, garnish with chopped tropical fruit or chopped cilantro and scallions.

YIELD: 2 SERVINGS (WITH POSSIBLE LEFTOVERS!)

Black Bean Salsa with Exotic Chips

1 can (15 ounces) **black beans,** drained

1 plum **tomato,** seeded and chopped

3 tablespoons finely chopped red **onion**

1 **jalapeño** pepper, seeded and finely chopped

1 clove **garlic,** finely chopped

Juice of 1 **lime**

A few dashes **hot sauce,** to taste

Salt, to taste

Chopped **cilantro** (optional)

1 bag (5 ounces) **plantain chips,** such as Goya brand or 1 bag root vegetable chips, such as Terra Chips brand, any variety

In a medium bowl, mix black beans, tomatoes, onions, peppers, garlic, lime juice, hot sauce, and salt. Garnish with cilantro (optional). Serve with plantain chips or fancy veggie chips for scooping.

YIELD: 2 & 1/2 CUPS SALSA

MENU BIG CITY BISTRO

~ COD WITH BURST GRAPE TOMATOES AND PARSLEY-MINT PESTO BROTH

~ FINGERLING POTATO CRISPS WITH HERBS

Cod with Burst Grape Tomatoes, Parsley-Mint Pesto Broth and Fingerling Potato Crisps with Herbs

You could get $40 a head for this plate! Nice!

POTATO CRISPS
2 large fingerling **potatoes**
1 tablespoon **extra-virgin olive oil** (evoo)
Salt and freshly ground black **pepper**, to taste
1 tablespoon chopped fresh **tarragon** or 1 teaspoon dried
1 tablespoon chopped fresh **chives** or 1 teaspoon dried
1 tablespoon chopped fresh flat-leaf **parsley**

FISH
1 pound thick, center-cut **cod** fillet, cut into 2 portions
Juice of 1/4 **lemon**
Salt and freshly ground black **pepper**, to taste
Extra-virgin olive oil (evoo), for drizzling
1/2 pint whole grape **tomatoes**

BROTH
1/3 cup fresh flat-leaf **parsley** (a couple handfuls)
1/4 cup **mint** leaves (a handful)
1 cup **chicken broth**
1 small **shallot** or 1/2 large shallot, coarsely chopped
Salt and freshly ground black **pepper**, to taste

3 tablespoons olive or vegetable **oil**, for frying
3 cloves **garlic**, gently cracked from skin and very thinly sliced

Preheat oven to 400°F.

Preheat a medium oven-safe skillet over high heat. If your skillet doesn't have an oven-safe handle, wrap it in two layers of foil to protect it.

Prick the potatoes 3 or 4 times each with a fork and cook them in the microwave for 5 minutes on high.

Pat cod dry, squeeze a little lemon juice over it, and season with salt. Drizzle fish with evoo.

When potatoes are just cool enough to handle, slice them lengthwise into 1/4-inch pieces. Coat them with evoo and salt and pepper. Arrange them on a cookie sheet in a single layer and roast them in the oven for 20 minutes. Do not move or turn them as they cook. Combine tarragon, chives, and parsley and reserve.

Add cod, seasoned side down, to preheated, very hot skillet and sear for 2 minutes. Drizzle tomatoes with evoo and season with salt and pepper. Add tomatoes to the fish and sear for 1 minute. Transfer pan to the oven and roast until fish if firm and opaque and tomatoes have all burst, 8 minutes.

Place parsley, mint, chicken broth, and shallots in food processor or blender, and purée. Transfer to small saucepot and bring to a simmer. Season the broth with salt and pepper.

Heat the frying oil in a small skillet over medium heat. Add sliced garlic to the hot oil and let it fry until crisp and golden brown, 3 to 5 minutes. Drain garlic chips on paper towel and reserve.

When the potatoes are very brown and crisp on the bottom side and tender on top, remove. Coat sliced potatoes liberally with the chopped tarragon, chives, and parsley.

Ladle warm pesto broth onto each dinner plate. Remove the fish from the oven. The bottom should be crisp and brown. Place the fish crispy-side up in pools of broth. Arrange the herb potato slices and tomatoes decoratively around the fish. Top the dish off with a scattering of garlic crisps and serve.

YIELD: 2 SERVINGS

MENU INSANELY GOOD ITALIAN BISTRO DINNER

~ PESTO TORTA

~ VEAL MILANESE

~ STRAWBERRIES WITH AMARETTO

Pesto Torta

This torta looks beautiful and will keep for up to four days, for snacking.

A drizzle **extra-virgin olive oil (evoo)**

4 pieces **sun-dried tomatoes** from a jar

4 leaves fresh **basil**

3 tubs (about 6 ounces each) **Boursin** cheese, or 2 tubs Alouette garlic and herb cheese, room temperature

1/4 cup store-bought sun-dried tomato **tapenade**

1/4 cup store-bought **pesto**

1 **baguette**, pre-sliced at the bread counter

Pour a little evoo in a small bowl and brush it around. Line the bowl with plastic wrap—the oil on the bowl will hold it in place. Add a drizzle of evoo to the bowl and brush it over the wrap. Arrange a pattern in the bottom of the dish using whole pieces of sun-dried tomatoes and whole basil leaves. (I arrange them like an open flower.) Add half the cheese to the bowl and smooth the top, pressing it into the bowl firmly. Next, layer in the sun-dried tomato spread, then add a layer of pesto. Carefully press the remaining cheese into place on top of the pesto and smooth the top. Place a serving plate over the bowl and invert the bowl. Hold on to the edges of the plastic wrap to release the cheese torta. Remove the plastic wrap. Arrange some sliced baguette alongside the torta. As you cut through the torta and spread it on the bread, you will get layers of cheese, sun-dried tomatoes, pesto, and more cheese.

YIELD: 1 POUND TORTA

COOKING 'ROUND THE CLOCK

Veal Milanese

This is a good item to make for company because you have the option of serving it at room temperature. In Italy you'll often find this dish on lunch buffets. The optional raw garlic in this dish may be too strong for some, but I love it!

2 boneless pieces of **veal loin** or shoulder (8–10 ounces each; about 1-inch thick)

Salt and freshly ground black **pepper**, to taste

3 or 4 tablespoons all-purpose **flour**

1 large **egg**, beaten

1 cup **bread crumbs** (eyeball it)

1/2 cup grated **Parmigiano** Reggiano or Romano cheese (a couple handfuls)

1/2 teaspoon freshly grated **nutmeg** (eyeball it)

Olive oil, for frying

3 small vine-ripened **tomatoes**

1/2 small to medium **onion**, chopped (about 1/2 cup)

1 small clove **garlic**, finely chopped (optional)

1 cup fresh **basil** leaves (15–20 leaves), torn or shredded

A drizzle **extra-virgin olive oil** (evoo)

Coarse **salt**, to taste

1/2 **lemon**, cut into wedges

Pound the veal 1 piece at a time between wax paper using a small heavy skillet or a mallet to 1/4-inch thickness. The pieces of veal will be thin and huge: each about 10 inches long and 6 inches wide. Season meat with salt and pepper. Set up an assembly line of shallow dishes: one with flour, one with beaten egg, one with bread crumbs combined with cheese and nutmeg.

Add a thin layer of oil to a very large skillet over medium heat. When oil is hot, add both pieces of veal. Cook until evenly golden, about 3 minutes on each side. Start chopping tomatoes for the raw sauce, keeping an eye on the veal.

Combine chopped tomatoes with onions, garlic (if desired), and basil and drizzle with evoo. Season with salt. Pile sauce onto cooked veal and serve with lemon wedges.

YIELD: 2 SERVINGS

Strawberries with Amaretto

1 pint **strawberries**, hulled and halved or sliced

1 tablespoon grated **orange** or lemon zest

2 teaspoons **sugar**

1/4 cup **Amaretto**

1 package **ladyfingers**

1 canister **whipped cream**

Sliced almonds, for garnish

Mix berries with zest, sugar, and Amaretto and let stand for at least 10 minutes. Line 2 dessert bowls with ladyfingers, covering the bottom and sides of the bowl to the top and gently molding them to the bowl. Divide the berries between the 2 bowls and top with a swirl of whipped cream and some sliced almonds.

YIELD: 2 SERVINGS

Big eats for the wee small hours.
Put together these yummy no-fuss
recipes with ingredients you
have on hand.

COOKING 'ROUND THE CLOCK

LATE-NITE
12 to 7
BITES

RACHAEL RAY
30-MINUTE MEALS

Tartines are like open-faced sandwiches: large, single slices of good-quality bread topped with vegetables, meats, and/or cheeses. They're a midnight-snack-lover's dream, because you can dress them up or down in a thousand ways in no time at all.

TARTINES: TOASTER-OVEN ARTS

~ **HAM AND CHEESE TARTINE WITH GREENS, ITALIAN STYLE**

~ **HAM AND CHEESE TARTINE WITH GREENS, FRENCH STYLE**

~ **TUNA CASSEROLE TARTINE**

~ **PÂTÉ TARTINE**

~ **BACON, LETTUCE, AVOCADO, AND TOMATO TARTINE**

~ **MEDITERRANEAN BLT TARTINE**

~ **CUPBOARD VEGETABLE TARTINE WITH CHEESE AND ANCHOVIES**

Ham and Cheese Tartine with Greens, Italian Style

1 large, thin slice good-quality **bread**

1 large clove **garlic**, cracked away from skin

1/4 pound **fontina** or provolone cheese, sliced

4 slices **prosciutto** di Parma

1 cup mixed **greens**, any variety

Extra-virgin olive oil (evoo), for drizzling

Salt and freshly ground black **pepper**, to taste

Preheat broiler in toaster oven or regular oven to high.

Toast bread until lightly browned, 1 minute on each side; leave broiler on. Rub toast with cracked garlic. Cover bread with cheese. Place bread on a baking sheet and put under broiler until cheese bubbles and is golden at edges, 1 to 3 minutes. Top with loose piles of prosciutto. Dress greens with a drizzle of evoo and some salt and pepper, and pile them on top of prosciutto.

YIELD: 1 SERVING

Ham and Cheese Tartine with Greens, French Style

1 large, thin slice good-quality **bread**

1 tablespoon **Dijon** mustard

1/4 pound **Gruyère** or Swiss cheese, shredded or sliced

2 or 3 thin slices vine-ripened **tomato**

3 deli slices boiled or baked **ham**

1 cup mixed baby **greens**

A splash of red wine **vinegar**

Extra-virgin olive oil (evoo), for drizzling

Salt and freshly ground black **pepper**, to taste

Preheat broiler in toaster oven or regular oven to high.

Toast bread 1 minute on each side and place on a baking sheet; leave broiler on. Spread toast with mustard and top with cheese, then return bread to broiler until cheese is lightly golden and bubbly, 1 to 3 minutes. Top the melted cheese with tomatoes and loosely piled ham. Dress greens with vinegar, evoo, salt, and pepper and pile on top of ham.

YIELD: 1 SERVING

INSIDE SCOOP

The Bread: Buy a whole loaf of whole-wheat, white, or multi-grain bread at a bakery counter and ask them to slice the bread lengthwise rather than across, to make long, rectangular slices, perfect for tartines. Keep this bread in your fridge and you can get two weeks of great snacking out of each loaf. Equally perfect for tartines are large, round loaves of country white, semolina, or sourdough bread. Keep the bread in an airtight bag in the refrigerator to get a long life out of each loaf.

Tuna Casserole Tartine

1 tablespoon **extra-virgin olive oil** (evoo) (once around the pan)

1/4 small **onion** or 1 shallot, chopped

4 fresh or marinated **mushrooms**, thinly sliced

1 can (6 ounces) **tuna** in oil or water, drained well

Salt and freshly ground black **pepper**, to taste

1/4 cup **cream** or half-and-half

2–3 tablespoons grated **Parmigiano** Reggiano or Romano cheese

A handful of frozen **peas**

1 large, thin slice good-quality **bread**

2 deli slices **Swiss** cheese

Preheat broiler in toaster oven or regular oven to high.

Heat a small skillet over medium heat. Add evoo, onions, and mushrooms; cook to soften, 3 minutes. Add tuna, cook 3 minutes more. Season with pepper, add cream, and simmer to reduce and thicken, 2 to 3 minutes. Add grated cheese and salt. Add peas and stir to combine; remove from heat.

Toast bread 1 minute on each side and place on a baking sheet. Spoon tuna casserole onto bread, mounding it all the way to the edges. Top tuna with Swiss cheese and return the bread to the oven. Cook until cheese has melted and browned at edges, 1 to 3 minutes.

YIELD: 1 SERVING

Pâté Tartine

1 large, thin slice good-quality **bread**

1 tablespoon stone-ground **mustard**

1/8 pound (2 or 3 ounces) country-style or mousse **pâté**

3 tablespoons chopped **cornichons** (finely chopped baby gherkins or dill pickles may be substituted)

2 tablespoons finely chopped **shallot** or onion

2 teaspoons drained **capers**

Freshly ground black **pepper**, to taste

Preheat broiler in toaster oven or regular oven and lightly toast bread 1 minute on each side.

Spread toast with mustard, then pâté. Top with cornichons, shallots, capers, and a few grinds of pepper.

YIELD: 1 SERVING

Bacon, Lettuce, Avocado, and Tomato Tartine

3 slices **bacon** or pancetta

1 large, thin slice good-quality **bread**

1 small, ripe **avocado**

1 small clove **garlic**

Coarse **salt** and freshly ground black **pepper**, to taste

Juice of 1/2 **lemon**

A few drops **hot sauce**, such as Tabasco

3–4 leaves green leaf or red leaf **lettuce** or romaine, coarsely chopped

Extra-virgin olive oil (evoo), for drizzling

1 small vine-ripened or plum **tomato**, sliced

Cook bacon in a small skillet or in the microwave until crisp.

Preheat broiler in toaster oven or a regular oven. Toast the bread 1 minute on each side.

Cut around avocado down to the pit with a sharp knife. Twist avocado halves and separate them. Whack the pit with the knife to get it out of the flesh. Scoop the avocado into a small bowl. Chop garlic, add a little salt, and mash it into a paste with the side of the knife. Add garlic paste to avocado with a few dashes of hot sauce. Add about 2 teaspoons of the lemon juice and stir to combine. Slather mashed avocado over the bread, mounding it up and covering the bread to the edges. Dress greens with a little lemon juice and evoo and pile them on top of the avocado. Slice tomato and season with salt and pepper. Cut cooked bacon slices in half and arrange them on greens. Arrange tomato slices on top of bacon and greens.

YIELD: 1 SERVING

Mediterranean BLT Tartine

Extra-virgin olive oil (evoo), for drizzling

3 slices **pancetta** or bacon

1 large, thin slice good-quality **bread**

1 small clove **garlic**, cracked away from skin

1/4 cup store-bought **pesto** or olive tapenade

3 or 4 leaves green leaf or red leaf **lettuce** or romaine, coarsely chopped

2 teaspoons lemon juice or red wine **vinegar**

Salt and freshly ground black **pepper**, to taste

Several leaves fresh **basil**, torn (optional)

1 small vine-ripened or plum **tomato**, sliced

Heat a small skillet over medium-high heat. Add a drizzle of evoo and the pancetta (if using bacon, cut slices in half). Cook pancetta until crisp, 2 or 3 minutes on each side. Drain on paper towels, let cool, and coarsely chop.

Preheat broiler in toaster oven or regular oven. Toast bread 1 minute on each side. Rub toast with cracked garlic. Spread pesto or tapenade evenly over toast.

Dress greens with lemon juice or vinegar and a drizzle of evoo, then season with salt and pepper. Mix in some basil leaves, if any on hand. Pile greens on toast and top with pancetta. Slice tomato and season with salt and pepper. Arrange tomatoes over pancetta.

YIELD: 1 SERVING

Cupboard Vegetable Tartine with Cheese and Anchovies

All the vegetables in this recipe come in jars. You can keep them on hand in the pantry and use them in any combination you choose.

1 large, thin slice good-quality **bread**

2 tablespoons store-bought **pesto** or olive tapenade

VEGETABLE CHOICES:

3–4 slices sliced marinated **eggplant**

1 roasted **red pepper**, drained and sliced

4–5 **marinated mushrooms**, drained and sliced

2–3 **sun-dried tomatoes** (soft, dry-packaged or in oil), drained and chopped

2 marinated **artichoke hearts** or artichoke hearts in water, drained and sliced

1/2 cup chopped **giardiniera** (Italian hot pickled vegetable mix), drained

TOPPINGS:

2–3 tablespoons chopped green or black **olives**

2–3 tablespoons chopped fresh **herbs** (whichever you have on hand—basil, parsley, oregano, thyme, or chives)

2–3 ounces fresh **goat cheese** or feta cheese, crumbled

3–4 **anchovies**, coarsely chopped (optional)

Preheat toaster oven broiler or regular broiler and toast bread 1 minute on each side.

Spread toast with pesto or tapenade, and top with any or all of the following vegetables: eggplant, roasted red pepper, marinated mushrooms, sun-dried tomatoes, artichoke hearts, giardiniera.

Garnish the bread with olives and fresh herbs. Top with liberal amounts of cheese and anchovies, if using.

YIELD: 1 SERVING

A QUICK ITALIAN BITE

Bread "Gnocchi" with Tomato and Basil

2 slices (1 & 1/2- to 2-inches thick) good-quality day-old Italian
   bread

1 tablespoon **extra-virgin olive oil** (evoo) (twice around the pan)

1 tablespoon **butter**

2 cloves **garlic**, finely chopped

Salt and freshly ground black **pepper**, to taste

1 cup **tomato sauce**

1 small plum **tomato**, seeded and chopped

A few leaves **basil**, torn

1/2 cup shredded **mozzarella**, smoked mozzarella, or provolone
   cheese

Preheat the broiler.

Heat a small skillet over medium heat. Chop bread into bite-size pieces.
Add evoo, butter, and garlic to pan. When butter has melted into oil, add
the bread. Season bread with salt and pepper and cook, tossing and
turning it in the garlic oil, 5 minutes. Add tomato sauce and tomatoes and
toss and turn to coat and combine. Transfer to a small casserole or dish,
cover with basil and cheese, and place under hot broiler or in toaster oven
until cheese browns and bubbles, 2 or 3 minutes.

YIELD: 1 SERVING

PITA-ZAS: MORE TOASTER-OVEN ARTS

~ GREEK PITA-ZA

~ PITA-ZA CROSTINI

~ HUMMUS PITA-ZA

~ GAZPACHO PITA-ZA

Greek Pita-za

1 **pita** bread

A handful baby **spinach**, arugula, or mixed greens

Extra-virgin olive oil (evoo), for drizzling

3 cherry or grape **tomatoes**, halved, or 1/2 vine-ripened tomato, chopped

3 tablespoons chopped red or white **onion**

3 tablespoons chopped pitted Kalamata **olives**

1/4 cup crumbled **feta** cheese

1 tablespoon fresh **oregano** or 1 teaspoon dried

Freshly ground black **pepper**, to taste

1/4 cup chopped seedless **cucumber** (a handful)

2 **pepperoncini**, chopped (optional)

A wedge of **lemon** (optional)

Preheat toaster oven or regular oven to 400°F.

Place pita on a baking tray. Combine greens with a drizzle of evoo. Pile greens on bread, working to edges. Top with tomatoes, onions, olives, feta, oregano, and pepper. Cook until bread is crisp on bottom and feta is brown at edges and has melted a little, 6 to 8 minutes. Remove pita to a plate and top with cucumber and pepperoncini (if using). Squeeze a little lemon juice over the top just before you eat, if desired.

YIELD: 1 SERVING

Pita-za Crostini

1 **pita** bread

3 tablespoons shredded **Asiago**, parmesan, or Italian 4-cheese blend

1 vine-ripened or plum **tomato**, chopped

2 tablespoons chopped white or red **onion**

1 small clove **garlic**, finely chopped

Extra-virgin olive oil (evoo), for drizzling

A handful chopped fresh flat-leaf **parsley** or torn basil leaves

Salt and freshly ground black **pepper**, to taste

Preheat toaster oven or regular oven to 400°F.

Place pita on a baking tray. Sprinkle with cheese and toast until bread is crisp and cheese is golden, 5 minutes. Combine tomatoes, onions, garlic, evoo, parsley, salt, and pepper and spoon over the crisp bread.

YIELD: 1 SERVING

Hummus Pita-za

1 **pita** bread

1/4 cup store-bought cracked chili pepper **hummus** or 40-spice hummus, such as Tribe of Two Sheiks brand

1/4 cup chopped seedless **cucumber**

1/2 small **tomato**, chopped

2 tablespoons chopped fresh **herbs**: dill, parsley, chives (use any or all)

Preheat toaster oven or regular oven to 400°F.

Place pita on a baking tray and cover with hummus. Bake until bread is crisp and hummus begins to brown, 7 to 10 minutes. Remove from oven and top with cucumbers, tomatoes, and herbs.

YIELD: 1 SERVING

Gazpacho Pita-za

1 **pita** bread

1/4 cup shredded or shaved **manchego**, sharp cheddar, or pecorino cheese

1 plum **tomato**, chopped

1/4 red or green **bell pepper**, chopped

3 tablespoons red or white **onion** or scallion, chopped

1 small clove **garlic**, chopped

2 teaspoons **hot sauce**, such as Tabasco

2 teaspoons **lemon** juice

Extra-virgin olive oil (evoo), for drizzling

Salt and freshly ground black **pepper**, to taste

Chopped fresh flat-leaf **parsley** or cilantro, for garnish (optional)

Preheat toaster oven or regular oven to 400°F.

Place pita on a baking tray. Top with cheese and bake until crisp, 7 to 10 minutes.

Combine tomatoes, bell peppers, onions, garlic, hot sauce, lemon juice, evoo, salt, and pepper. Top pita with mixture and garnish with chopped parsley or cilantro, if desired.

YIELD: 1 SERVING

QUESADILLA IN A HURRY

~ QUESADILLA PIZZA

~ GRILLED GREEN QUESADILLA WITH BRIE AND HERBS

Quesadilla Pizza

2 flour **tortillas** (8-inch diameter)

1 cup shredded **manchego**, cheddar, Monterey Jack, or pepper-Jack cheese

1 cup chipotle **salsa** or salsa verde

1 **scallion**, chopped

1/2 cup chopped cooked **chicken**, pork, chorizo, or shrimp

Preheat a toaster oven to 400°F.

Place a tortilla on a baking tray and top with half the cheese, then another tortilla. Bake 5 minutes. Spread salsa over top tortilla, working it to the edges, and cover the salsa with the remaining cheese, the scallions, and chopped meat or shrimp. Bake until cheese has melted and bottom tortilla is brown and crisp, 5 to 7 minutes.

YIELD: 1 SERVING

Grilled Green Quesadilla with Brie and Herbs

A drizzle of **extra-virgin olive oil** (evoo)

1 large **spinach wrap** (12-inch diameter) (available on dairy aisle)

1/4 pound **brie** with herbs, sliced

2 tablespoons chopped fresh **chives** or 1 teaspoon dried

2 tablespoons chopped fresh **tarragon** or 1 teaspoon dried

Heat a large nonstick skillet over medium-high heat. Brush or rub a drizzle of evoo on tortilla. Char the wrap a minute, then flip. Arrange a layer of sliced brie with herbs across half of flour wrap. Sprinkle cheese with chives and tarragon, fold quesadilla in half, covering cheese. Lightly press down on quesadilla, turn, and cook 30 seconds longer. Cut into wedges and serve.

YIELD: 1 SERVING

POLISH SMASH

Mashed Potatoes, Sausage, and Peas

Thanks go out to my good friend Emily for this one: When she went to her grandma's as a kid, she had a yummy concoction similar to this recipe. When she returned home, she told her mom all about it. Mom thought it quite gross, indeed! Me? Love at first virtual-bite as I cooked it up in my head!

1 large baking **potato**

3 tablespoons **butter**, divided

1/4 cup **milk** or half-and-half (eyeball it)

1 **scallion**, chopped, or 2 tablespoons chopped chives (optional)

1 teaspoon dried **dill** (optional)

Salt and freshly ground black **pepper**, to taste

1/2 tablespoon **extra-virgin olive oil** (evoo) or vegetable oil (half a turn around the pan)

Sausage: 1/4 pound kielbasa or 2 hot dogs or 1 knockwurst or bratwurst, chopped into bite-size pieces

1 cup frozen **peas**

Prick potato several times with tines of a fork and microwave on high for 8 minutes. Let stand until cool enough to handle, 3 to 5 minutes.

Cut potato in half and scoop all the flesh into a small bowl. Mash with 2 tablespoons butter and about 1/4 cup milk. Add scallions or chives and dill, if desired. Season with salt and pepper.

Heat a small skillet over medium-high heat. Add oil and the remaining tablespoon butter. When butter has melted into oil, add chopped sausage. Fry meat in pan until crisp at edges and lightly browned, 2 or 3 minutes. Add potatoes to the pan and smash them together with the sausage. Add peas and continue to cook another 2 or 3 minutes, to get potatoes good and hot again and heat the peas through.

YIELD: 1 SERVING

DINER CLASSIC 1

Deli Hash

1 medium red-skinned **potato** or 1 small white potato

2 tablespoons **extra-virgin olive oil** (evoo) (twice around the pan)

1/4 pound deli-sliced **corned beef**, pastrami, or smoked turkey, finely chopped

1/4 small **onion**, finely chopped

1/4 small **red bell pepper**, finely chopped

Salt and freshly ground black **pepper**, to taste

1 rounded tablespoon deli **mustard**

A few drops **hot sauce**, such as Tabasco

1 tablespoon **butter**

1 large **egg**

Prick skin of potato with a fork in several places and microwave on high 5 minutes; let stand 2 minutes.

Meanwhile, heat a medium skillet over medium to medium-high heat. Add evoo, then meat, onions, and peppers. Season with salt and pepper and cook the meat and veggies 5 minutes. Remove potato from microwave and chop it into small pieces and add it to meat and veggies. Stir in mustard and hot sauce; add salt and pepper and cook hash 5 minutes more.

Heat a small nonstick skillet over medium-low heat. Melt butter in pan and fry egg: 1 minute for over easy, a few minutes longer for over hard. Pile hash onto a plate and top with egg.

YIELD: 1 SERVING

DINER CLASSIC 2

Midnight Monte Cristo

2 slices white or whole wheat **bread**

1/8 pound sliced **Swiss**, fontina, or Gruyère cheese

2 or 3 slices **prosciutto**, prosciutto cotto, or other ham or smoked turkey

1 large **egg**

A splash of **milk** or half-and-half

1 **scallion**, finely chopped

Salt and freshly ground black **pepper**

A drizzle of **extra-virgin olive oil** (evoo)

1/2 tablespoon **butter**

Make a sandwich out of 2 slices bread and the cheese and meat. Heat a small nonstick skillet over medium to medium-high heat. Beat egg with milk, scallions, salt, and pepper. Add a drizzle of evoo and the butter to the skillet. When butter has melted into evoo, coat sandwich on both sides in egg mixture and place in hot pan. Cook sandwich until evenly golden and cheese has melted, 3 minutes on each side.

YIELD: 1 SERVING

BREAKFAST AT MIDNIGHT

~ VEGGIE SCRAMBLES WITH PESTO

~ SALAMI SCRAMBLES

~ EGG SCRAMBLE WITH SALMON

~ HOT DOG SCRAMBLES

~ LATE-NIGHT HOME FRIES WITH PEPPERS AND ONIONS

~ GREEN RANCH-HAND EGGS

~ HUEVOS RANCHEROS

~ MEXICAN COFFEE

~ NESTERS

Veggie Scrambles with Pesto

2 tablespoons **extra-virgin olive oil** (evoo) (twice around the pan)

1/4 small **onion,** chopped

1/4 small **red bell pepper,** chopped

1/2 cup frozen **peas**

3 **eggs**

Salt and freshly ground black **pepper,** to taste

2 rounded teaspoonfuls store-bought **pesto**

Heat a medium skillet over medium to medium-high heat. Add evoo, then onions and peppers. Cook 3 minutes, then add peas and cook another minute or 2. Whisk eggs with salt and pepper. Add eggs to veggies and scramble in the pan to desired doneness. Remove from heat and stir in pesto.

YIELD: 1 SERVING

Salami Scrambles

1 tablespoon **extra-virgin olive oil** (evoo) (once around the pan)

1/8 pound (5–6 slices) deli-sliced **salami** (Genoa, hard, sopressata, or hot sopressata), chopped

1 clove **garlic**, chopped

1 **scallion**, chopped, or 2 tablespoons chopped onion

1 plum **tomato** or 3-4 cherry tomatoes, chopped, or 3 tablespoons chopped sun-dried tomatoes

3 large **eggs**

2 rounded tablespoons crumbled garlic and herb **cheese** (Boursin or Alouette brands), crumbled feta cheese, or crumbled herb goat cheese

Salt and freshly ground black **pepper**

Chopped fresh flat-leaf **parsley**, for garnish

Chopped or torn **basil**, for garnish

Heat a medium nonstick skillet over medium heat. Add evoo and salami. Cook salami until it renders some fat and starts to turn a deep burgundy color, 2 minutes. Add garlic and stir 30 seconds, then add scallions and cook a minute or 2 more. Add tomatoes then cook another minute or 2. Beat eggs with cheese, a little salt and a generous amount of pepper. Add eggs to pan and scramble with other ingredients. Top with parsley and/or basil to garnish, then serve.

YIELD: 1 SERVING

Egg Scramble with Salmon

3 **eggs**, beaten

2 or 3 tablespoons garlic and herb **cheese**, such as Boursin or Alouette, or cream cheese

1 **scallion**, chopped or 2 tablespoons chopped chives

Salt and freshly ground black **pepper**, to taste

A few drops **hot sauce**, such as Tabasco

2 tablespoons **butter** or extra-virgin olive oil (evoo)

1/4 cup frozen **peas** (optional)

2 ounces (3 slices) **smoked salmon**, cut into strips

Whisk eggs with cheese and scallion and season with salt, pepper, and hot sauce. The cheese will be in small bits mixed throughout the egg. It looks odd, but it all melts together as eggs cook.

Preheat a small or medium nonstick skillet over medium heat. Add butter or evoo, heat, then add eggs. Stir in peas, if using. Scramble eggs to desired consistency and top with ribbons of sliced salmon.

YIELD: 1 SERVING

Hot Dog Scrambles

1/2 tablespoon vegetable **oil** or olive oil (half a turn around the pan)

1 **hot dog**, any variety, chopped

3 **eggs**, beaten

Salt and freshly ground black **pepper**, to taste

2 teaspoons **hot sauce**, such as Tabasco (eyeball it)

SPECIAL SAUCE

2 tablespoons **ketchup**

2 tablespoons **salsa** or chili sauce

2 teaspoons pickle **relish**

2 tablespoons finely chopped **onions** or scallions

Heat a small nonstick skillet over medium-high heat. Add oil, then chopped hot dog; fry until hot dog is crisp at edges and lightly browned, 3 minutes. Add eggs, reduce heat to medium-low, and season with salt, pepper, and hot sauce. Scramble to desired doneness.

Make the sauce: Combine ketchup, salsa or chili sauce, relish, and onions. Transfer eggs to a plate and top with sauce.

YIELD: 1 SERVING

Late-Night Home Fries with Peppers and Onions

Make this recipe with any of the Late-Night Scrambles.

1 large baking **potato**
1 tablespoon **extra-virgin olive oil** (evoo)
1 tablespoon **butter**
1/2 medium **onion,** chopped
1/2 **green bell pepper,** seeded and chopped
1 tablespoon **grill seasoning** blend, such as Montreal Steak
    Seasoning by McCormick
1 teaspoon sweet **paprika**

Prick a large baking potato several times with a fork and microwave on high for 8 minutes. Remove and let sit until cool enough to handle, 3 to 5 minutes.

Heat a small nonstick skillet over medium-high heat. Add evoo, then butter. Coarsely chop potato and add it to the skillet with onions and peppers. Season with grill seasoning and paprika and cook until browned and peppers and onions are tender, but still have a bite to them, 7 or 8 minutes.

YIELD: 1 SERVING

Green Ranch-Hand Eggs

1 cup (half a 15-ounce can) **black beans**

1 teaspoon **ground chipotle** or chili powder or cumin (1/3 of a palmful)

1 teaspoon **hot sauce**, such as Tabasco (several drops)

Extra-virgin olive oil (evoo), for drizzling

1 large **egg**

Salt and freshly ground black **pepper**, to taste

1/2 cup tomatillo **salsa** (salsa verde or green salsa), any brand

1/2 cup shredded **manchego** or sharp cheddar cheese (a couple of handfuls)

1 flour **tortilla** (6-inch diameter)

Chopped **cilantro** or chopped fresh flat-leaf parsley, for garnish

Finely chopped **scallions**, chives, or red onions, for garnish

Sour cream or plain yogurt, for garnish

Pour beans into a small skillet or microwave-safe bowl. Add ground chipotle and hot sauce. Heat beans over medium-low heat on the stove to warm through. For microwave, cover beans loosely with plastic, cook 30 seconds, stir, and return to microwave for another 30 seconds. Let stand.

Heat a small nonstick skillet or griddle over medium-low heat. When hot, drizzle pan with evoo and add egg. Cook egg gently to desired doneness—1 minute for easy, a bit longer for over hard. Season egg with salt and pepper.

Meanwhile, remove lid from the salsa jar and place jar in the microwave; warm through, 45 seconds on high.

Spoon warm salsa over the egg once you turn it over. Place shredded cheese on top. Cover the pan loosely with an aluminum foil tent to melt cheese.

If you have a gas stove, heat and blister the tortilla by holding it with tongs over the open flame of a burner, 15 to 20 seconds on each side. Otherwise, warm tortilla in a dry hot skillet over high heat 20 to 30 seconds on each side.

To assemble, place tortilla on a plate. Top with a generous spoonful of warm black beans; top beans with fried egg, salsa, and cheese. Finish it off with a sprinkle of cilantro or parsley; chopped scallions, chives, or red onion; and sour cream or yogurt.

YIELD: 1 SERVING

Huevos Rancheros

1 cup (half a 16-ounce can) **refried beans**

2 teaspoons **hot sauce**, such as Tabasco

1 small flour **tortilla** (6-inch diameter)

1 tablespoon **extra-virgin olive oil** (evoo) (once around the pan)
or 1 tablespoon butter

1 large **egg**

Salt and freshly ground black **pepper**, to taste

1/4 pound (4 ounces) **manchego** cheese or smoked cheddar
cheese, shredded

1/2 cup **enchilada sauce** or chipotle salsa

Place beans in a small bowl and stir in hot sauce. Cover loosely with plastic and cook in the microwave on high 45 seconds. Stir beans and cook another 30 seconds, until hot. Let stand.

Heat a small skillet over medium heat. Add tortilla to dry skillet and cook a minute or 2 on each side to soften and blister it, then place it on a plate. Add evoo or butter to skillet and fry egg to desired doneness, seasoning it with salt and pepper. Top egg with shredded cheese. Spread beans on tortilla then slide egg and cheese on top. Pour enchilada sauce or salsa over completed dish. You can use the sauce at room temperature, or you can heat it in the skillet you used for the egg, 30 seconds to 1 minute.

YIELD: 1 SERVING

Mexican Coffee

Good with either the Green Ranch-Hand Eggs or Huevos Rancheros, preceding.

4 scoops or rounded tablespoons ground **coffee beans**

1 scoop or rounded tablespoon **cocoa powder**

1/4 teaspoon ground **cinnamon**, plus a sprinkle for garnish

4 shots **coffee liqueur**, such as Kahlúa

1 canister **whipped cream**

Place coffee, cocoa, and cinnamon in the filter of a coffee maker. Make 4 cups of coffee. Pour 2 shots coffee liqueur in the bottom of a coffee mug. Pour in up to 2 cups of the Mexican mocha-cinnamon coffee. Top off the mug with a generous swirl of whipped cream and garnish with another sprinkle of cinnamon. Repeat.

YIELD: 2 BIG MUGFULS

Nesters

Bird in a nest, or fried egg in bread, is my favorite late-night snack, and I make that bird sing many different tunes, depending on what's in the fridge!

2 tablespoons **extra-virgin olive oil** (evoo) (twice around the pan)
1 clove **garlic,** cracked
1 slice (2 inches thick) good-quality day-old Italian **bread**
A handful of grated **Parmigiano** Reggiano or Romano cheese
1 large **egg**
Salt and freshly ground black **pepper,** to taste

FILLING CHOICES:
Anchovy fillets
Roasted red pepper, cut into strips
Chopped **hot peppers**
Chopped **salami**
Chopped **ham**
Chopped **olives**
Chopped fresh **herbs** (any kind)
A spoonful of store-bought **pesto** or tapenade
Chopped fresh **tomato**
Chopped **scallions**

Heat a small skillet over medium heat. Add evoo and garlic. Make a "nest": Remove about 2 inches of the bread at the center. Sprinkle cheese over the bread and place it in the pan cheese side down. The cheese will brown in the oil and stick to the bread. Turn bread over and drop the egg into the nest. Season the bird in the nest with salt and pepper and add any additional fillings of your choice—2 or 3 tablespoons of any chopped ingredient will fit in nicely. Cover pan with an aluminum foil tent and let the bird sit in nest 3 to 5 minutes to cook yolk to desired doneness.

YIELD: 1 SERVING

CRAZY ABOUT CHEESE

~ WELSH RAREBIT: A MAN'S FONDUE

~ INSTANT CHILI CON QUESO: A TEXAN'S FONDUE

~ ITALIAN HUMMUS AND EASY CHEESY SNACK

Welsh Rarebit: A Man's Fondue

Women who eat like men enjoy this, too—I'm one of 'em!

1 & 1/2 cups (half a 10-ounce sack) shredded sharp yellow cheddar cheese (preshredded is available on dairy aisle)

1 tablespoon butter, cut into pieces

A healthy splash of good lager beer

1 rounded teaspoon Dijon mustard

1 teaspoon Worcestershire sauce (several drops)

1 teaspoon hot sauce, such as Tabasco (several drops)

Salt and freshly ground black pepper, to taste

4 slices whole-grain bread, toasted and quartered corner to corner

Chopped anchovies, for garnish (optional)

Chopped green apple, for garnish (optional)

Heat cheese, butter, and beer in a saucepan over low heat, stirring, until cheese melts and mixture is smooth, about 5 minutes. Stir in mustard, Worcestershire, hot sauce, salt, and pepper. Spread the bread pieces out over a large plate and pour the sauce all over, leaving some exposed bread edges to grab on to. (Think of it as bread nachos.) If you are a brave eater (like me), top with chopped anchovies and/or green apples.

YIELD: 1 SERVING

Instant Chili con Queso: A Texan's Fondue

I cannot believe I am putting this recipe in a cookbook, as it could hardly be considered a recipe at all, but everyone has his or her guilty pleasures in life—this is mine. And yup, I use canned chili; I hide mine way in the back of the pantry.

1 can (15 ounces) store-bought **chili**
1 brick (3 ounces) **cream cheese,** cut into pieces
2 **scallions,** chopped
2 tablespoons chopped **cilantro** (optional)
Pretzel rods or corn chips, for dipping

Place chili, cream cheese, scallions, and cilantro (if using) in a small pot over low heat and cook until hot and cheese melts to combine with chili. Transfer to a bowl and serve with pretzel rods and/or chips for dipping.

YIELD: 2 SERVINGS

Italian Hummus and Easy Cheesy Snack

1 can (15 ounces) **garbanzo beans** (chickpeas), drained

1 clove **garlic,** cracked away from skin

Juice of 1/2 **lemon**

1 teaspoon crushed **red pepper flakes**

2–3 tablespoons fresh **rosemary** or thyme leaves

2–3 tablespoons **extra-virgin olive oil** (evoo) (eyeball it)

Coarse **salt,** to taste

1 wheel (5 ounces) **Boursin** cheese with garlic and herbs

1/4 cup store-bought **pesto**

1 package **flat breads** or Melba toasts, any flavor

In a food processor, combine garbanzos, garlic, lemon juice, red pepper flakes, and rosemary or thyme; turn processor on. Stream in evoo to combine and stop processing when a smooth, hummus-like consistency forms, 1 minute. Add salt and pulse-grind into the dip. Transfer dip to a small bowl.

Unwrap Boursin on a plate and cover with pesto sauce. Place Italian hummus alongside and surround with flat breads or toasts.

YIELD: 2 SERVINGS

Who's your
friend at
2AM?
Patty.

PATTY TIME

~ ALL-AMERICAN PATTY MELTS

~ ITALIAN-AMERICAN SAUSAGE PATTY MELTS

All-American Patty Melts

1/2 pound ground **sirloin**

1 rounded tablespoon dill pickle **relish**

1 tablespoon **steak sauce**

1/2 tablespoon **grill seasoning** blend, such as Montreal Steak Seasoning by McCormick

1 teaspoon sweet **paprika**

A drizzle of **extra-virgin olive oil** (evoo)

2 tablespoons **butter,** divided

1 medium **onion,** thinly sliced

4 slices rye, white, or pumpernickel **bread**

4 deli slices **Swiss** cheese

Heat a large nonstick skillet over medium-high heat. Mix meat with relish, steak sauce, grill seasoning, and paprika. Divide meat and form into 2 large, thin patties. Add evoo to pan and cook burgers 3 or 4 minutes on each side. Take patties out and add another drizzle of evoo and 1 tablespoon butter to the pan. When butter has melted into oil, fry onions until just tender, 5 minutes. Slide onions onto patties.

Return pan to the stove and add the remaining tablespoon butter and 2 slices of bread. Top each bread slice with a slice of cheese, a patty with onions, and another slice of cheese. Set remaining slices bread into place on the top of each sandwich and press the patty melts together. Cook 2 or 3 minutes on each side to set the sandwich and toast the bread. Cut sandwiches from corner to corner.

YIELD: 2 SERVINGS

Italian-American Sausage Patty Melts

2 tablespoons **extra-virgin olive oil** (evoo)

2 Italian sweet or hot **sausage patties** (1/2 pound) (available packaged in meat case)

1/2 **bell pepper**, thinly sliced, or 1 cubanelle (Italian long sweet) pepper, halved, seeded and sliced

1/2 small **onion**, thinly sliced

Salt and freshly ground black **pepper**, to taste

1/2 teaspoon crushed **red pepper flakes**

1 tablespoon **butter**

4 thin slices Italian **bread**

4 deli slices **provolone** cheese

1 cup marinara, **pizza sauce**, or tomato sauce

Heat a medium nonstick skillet over medium-high heat. Add one tablespoon evoo and the sausage patties. Cook patties 4 minutes on each side and remove from pan. Add another tablespoon evoo and the bell peppers, onions, salt, pepper, and pepper flakes. Cook until veggies are tender, but still have a bite to them, 5 minutes.

Pile veggies on the patties and return pan to the stove. Add butter and let it melt. Add 2 slices bread, top each with a slice of cheese, a sausage patty, some peppers and onions, another slice of cheese, then the remaining slices of bread. Press and turn patty melts 2 or 3 minutes on each side. Warm a cup of marinara, pizza sauce, or tomato sauce in microwave, 1 & 1/2 minutes on high. Cut sandwiches corner to corner and serve with sauce for dipping.

YIELD: 2 SERVINGS

A LATE-NIGHT PASTA

I knew my boyfriend was the man to marry when I asked him what he would like for his birthday dinner the first year we were together. I offered up lobster, steak, fine foods of all nationalities, to which he replied: "Can I just have some of your carbonara?" Whoa! I was right about him because today we are engaged.

Carbonara is bacon and egg pasta, a true classic from Italian cuisine. This is the food of the people! I never order it out because everyone messes with it: They add cream, mushrooms, ham—all kinds of stuff that simply does not belong.

Yes, I acknowledge that this dish is heavy and bad for you, especially when eaten in copious amounts late at night, and I know, I have included this in other books, but a late-night collection could never be complete without my carbonara!

The Only Recipe You Need: Carbonara

Salt and freshly ground black **pepper,** to taste
1 pound **rigatoni**
1/4 cup **extra-virgin olive oil** (evoo) (4 times around the pan)
1/4 pound **pancetta,** chopped
1 teaspoon crushed **red pepper flakes** (1/3 of a palmful)
5 or 6 cloves **garlic,** chopped
1/2 cup dry white **wine**
2 large **egg yolks**
1/2 cup grated **Romano** cheese, such as Locatelli
A handful of finely chopped fresh flat-leaf **parsley,** for garnish (optional)

Put a large pot of water on to boil. Add a liberal amount of salt and rigatoni; cook to al dente, about 8 minutes.

Meanwhile, heat a large skillet over medium heat. Add evoo and pancetta. Brown pancetta 2 minutes. Add red pepper flakes and garlic and cook 2 to 3 minutes more. Add wine and stir up all the pan drippings.

Beat yolks, then add 1 large ladleful (about 1/2 cup) of the pasta cooking water. This tempers the eggs and keeps them from scrambling when added to the pasta.

Drain pasta well and add it directly to the skillet with pancetta and oil. Pour the egg mixture over the pasta. Toss rapidly to coat the pasta without cooking the egg. Remove pan from heat and add a big handful of cheese, lots of pepper, and a little salt. Continue to toss and turn the pasta until it soaks up egg mixture and thickens, 1 to 2 minutes. Garnish with parsley, if desired, and extra cheese. Eating this out of the pan or one large bowl with 2 forks is extra-sexy!

YIELD: 2 HUGE SERVINGS, WITH SOME OR NONE LEFT OVER (USUALLY THIS RECIPE MAKES 6 SERVINGS, BUT LATE AT NIGHT, WHEN NO ONE CAN SEE US, WE CAN EAT AS MUCH AS WE WANT!)

Other Books by Rachael Ray

30-Minute Meals

The Open House Cookbook

Comfort Foods

Veggie Meals

30-Minute Meals 2

Get Togethers

$40 a Day

Cooking Rocks!

Published by

Lake Isle Press, Inc.